THE NATURE OF THE EARLY CHURCH

The Nature
of
The Early Church

By

ERNEST F. SCOTT, D.D.

NEW YORK
Charles Scribner's Sons
1941

PREFACE

The book of Acts was written before the end of the first century, and has been followed by innumerable works on the history of the church. It is strange, however, that while the subject has been studied minutely in all its phases and from every conceivable point of view, the question has seldom been raised of what the church is, in its essential nature. The importance, or even the possibility, of this question has been recognized only in our own day, and various answers to it have been put forward. None of them, it seems to the present writer, is fully adequate. The church, however it may resemble other societies, ancient or modern, is a unique creation, and can be explained only from something unique in the Christian message. An attempt is made in this book to determine how the church was related to the message, as it was understood by the first disciples, in the days immediately following the Lord's departure. It was then that the church arose, and the secret of its formative idea must be sought in that crucial period when it came into being.

The primitive church often has been compared to a tiny rill which was expanded in the course of time by many tributaries until it grew into a mighty river. This analogy is altogether misleading, for in a real sense the church was most fully itself at the very outset. The later movement becomes intelligible only when we go back to that first community which gave aim and motive to all that happened afterwards. It has been impossible, therefore, to limit the enquiry to that brief period with which it is immediately concerned. The problem of the primitive church cannot but broaden out into that of the church as it has always been, and still is today. This will account for much in the book that is not entirely relevant to a strictly historical enquiry.

Amidst the terrible events of the present there may seem to be little place for this investigation of an obscure chapter in the history of the past. The author has felt, however, that in this time when our Christian civilization is in peril its foundations need to be re-examined and tested. The church is the very symbol of those interests which the free nations are struggling to preserve, and there is a practical value in all effort to understand its meaning.

E. F. Scott.

June, 1941

CONTENTS

CHAPTER I

THE SIGNIFICANCE OF THE PRIMITIVE CHURCH

The Christian religion, from the beginning, has identified itself with a community. Before it had any formal creed it found expression in a group of men and women who had followed Jesus in his lifetime and now waited for his return. This group, when it first comes into our view, was made up of a hundred and twenty people, settled in Jerusalem. It steadily grew in numbers and extended its mission over Palestine, then into Syria, Asia Minor and the Western lands. In process of time it became the world-wide church.

It is customary to speak of the church as an institution, but this term is inadequate and misleading. It suggests a society which was formed deliberately, like a club or a business company, with a clearly defined object. The study of church history has been largely vitiated by this underlying assumption. Attempts are made to discover why the church was instituted, and what rules and ordinances were imposed on it. Questions are raised as to whether this institution was necessary, and if so, whether it has now served its purpose and needs to be replaced by something different. The church, however, was not instituted but arose spontaneously, and for some time was hardly conscious of its own existence. It has its true analogy, not in a society created of set purpose, but in a nation. We do not think of Rome or England or America as institutions. They grew of their own accord out of the association of people who were kindred in blood and had the same language and traditions. The nation was formed by a natural process, just as much as the rivers and forests of the land. This was no less true of the church. It was apparent even to pagans that the strange community which had sprung up among them was not one of the formal societies of which there were many in that time. They spoke of the Christians as "this new race of men." An alien people had arisen and was threatening all established rights.

The church is the Christian nation, and no other has had a history so varied and continuous. Our attention is too often absorbed by the mere succession of events, the outstanding leaders, the enterprises that have been achieved from time to time. We are now learning that the real interest even of ordinary history has little to do with these things, when they are taken by themselves. Events are important only as they serve to manifest or to shape the character of the people. We desire to know not so much what happened to them as what they are, and what have been their motives and purposes. This is still more true of the history of the church. Behind all the outward vicissitudes there is an outlook which always has been essentially the same. What is its nature? When we try to determine its ultimate meaning, what is this society which we call the church?

This question as a rule is left unanswered. We are content to know that after Jesus himself had departed those who believed in him united in carrying on his work, and it seems hardly necessary to enquire why they did so. Our concern is not with the dim origins of the Christian community but with the mature results. In the study of English history we do not linger over the vague migrations of Jutes and Angles in forgotten centuries. It may be admitted that without those obscure preliminaries nothing could have followed; but it is enough to know that somehow they took place and that the scene was thus prepared for the true history. In much the same manner we assume the beginnings of the church.

This is our attitude, too, with regard to its nature and function. For most people it is only a familiar part of the social order into which they were born. If they were pressed to define its purpose they would say that besides the ordinary needs men have a need for religion. They might be satisfied with private devotion, but the instinct of men is to work together, and they therefore associate in their religious life. As a result there has grown up a great society, of which the central object is worship, but which also takes on itself many other duties, connected, more or less directly, with the service of God. The church is the guardian of morality. It devotes itself to works of beneficence. It brings its members into friendly intercourse with each other. In our time, when races and classes are in acute conflict, it works for mutual understanding. It insists that every nation should treat the others justly, that labour should have its due reward, that laws should be humane and equitable. If it were not for the church all human relations would be at the mercy of self-interest, as in pagan times, but this great organization upholds the higher standards, and has therefore a necessary place in the life of the civilized world.

No one would deny that all this is true. The church is a great society in which it is possible for all men of good will to unite their forces and defend the cause of justice and brotherhood in the name of Christ. It is also in a real sense the means of salvation. Partaking in its worship men are brought into communion with Christ. They are touched with the regenerating influence which flowed from him, and has been transmitted through the long succession of his faithful people. But when all this is said we have not fully explained the church. It is not merely an organization like others, though working for beneficent ends and serving as a channel for the Christian life. It is different in kind from any other society. In order to understand it we have to consider, not so much its activities, moral and social and religious, as the idea which lies at the heart of it.

For this purpose it is necessary to go back to its very beginning. If only we can determine what was in the minds of the first disciples we may hope for some insight into the radical meaning of the church. In all the later effort that first intention has been the vital principle, although it has been so complicated with other interests that it is often difficult to trace. To apprehend it in its simplicity we need to return to the earliest days. This is true, in some measure, of every human society. A nation at the height of its power cherishes the memory of its beginnings, not merely out of a pious sentiment, but in order to explain to itself what has followed. In that remote past it gets down to the bedrock. Here were the conditions which gave it being, and which, in the last resort, must decide its destiny. A social or religious order reveres its founders. They worked on a small scale but for that reason were not distracted from their main purpose. Their memory is the compass by which their successors must continue to steer. In a more definite sense, however, we learn the meaning of the church through the primitive community. The beginnings of a nation are usually shrouded in darkness; nothing can be surely known of the actions of the pioneers and the motives which prompted them. Of the primitive church we know at least the essential facts. We know, too, that the first believers were the immediate disciples of Jesus, and were trying to put into effect what they had learned from him. There is no need to weave myths about them and credit them with motives of which they were not themselves aware. The evidence of their purpose is clearly there, in the recorded message of Jesus.

In all times it has been recognized that the church must study the example of the early days, and seek, if possible, to follow it. Too often, however, a false value has been placed on this example. It has been assumed that in all matters of government and institution the church must model itself on the primitive community. For that brief period at the beginning the church was uncorrupted. It guided itself in all respects by the instruction of Christ himself, and the one test of a true church is its similarity to that primitive one. On this point ecclesiastical controversy has always turned. Each denomination has sought to make out that it alone has remained faithful to the original model. The church of the Apostles was Episcopal or Presbyterian or Congregational, or was more akin to such irregular sects as the Plymouth Brethren or the Salvation Army. Every type of religious organization can be shown, without much difficulty, to have resemblances to the church of the New Testament. But we are now learning to see that all this discussion is beside the mark. The primitive model was one which never can be reproduced, for it answered to conditions which were altogether unique. The community had not yet called itself a church. It had no set order or government. It placed itself wholly under the control of the Spirit, which resided in the group as a whole and in each individual member. Such a community was possible only at the very beginning, when the church was small and was fired with a high enthusiasm. Even within the first year or two the primitive model had to be abandoned, and to return to it now could lead to no other result than sheer anarchy. We cannot revive the New Testament church, nor is this desirable. Jesus himself laid down no directions as to how his followers were to order their society. He only gave them a task to fulfil, and left them to discover for themselves how they might do so most effectually. Again and again the church must organize itself afresh, to meet the requirements of each new time, and according as it is best fitted to the time it gives meaning and reality to its message.

What we need to discover from the study of that first community is not how it was organized and administered, but rather why it came into existence. A society was formed which has ever since maintained itself and has spread over the earth; what was it supposed to be? From its later history this question cannot very well be answered. There was a period in the Middle Ages when the church was everything, and amidst the multiplicity of its interests it is hardly possible to distinguish a central one. In our own time the church is constantly under rebuke for neglecting one duty or another, and can never affirm with certainty that this does not lie within its province. But at the outset there was none of this confusion. The church had its task clearly marked out for it. Its members were possessed with a great conviction which took concrete form in their fellowship. What was this conviction?

It is obvious that the question has an urgent practical importance. The first thing necessary in planning out a journey is to fix the destination. No enterprise can be properly carried through unless the object is known and tenaciously kept in mind. Yet the church, for the most part, has only the vaguest sense of what it is seeking to do. Most of its errors are to be set down, not to moral failure or want of intelligence, but simply to confusion of aim. If it is to fulfil the purpose for which it exists it must first know what that purpose is; and this it can do only by reminding itself of how it began. It had then a clear vision of its calling, and in the light of that vision it must keep itself in the right way.

What do we know, then, about the primitive church? The record might seem to be limited to a few bare facts, preserved for the most part in the book of Acts. Writing after an interval of fifty or sixty years, the author has done his best to collect the stray memories of the primitive time. When allowance is made for his difficulties he has performed his task well. Some of his material would seem to be taken from actual documents. Few records of this kind can have been available, and they would be little more than scanty jottings; but such as they were Luke has sought them out and made the most of them. He has also woven into his narrative a number of reminiscences which had come down by various channels and sometimes had been coloured and worn out of shape in the process. Luke has wisely preserved them just as they had come to him, for the fanciful additions were themselves significant, reflecting, as they do, the ideas and beliefs which were habitual to the first disciples. For the general picture he is himself responsible. He has often been charged with credulity, with writing for effect, with substituting romance for history, but perhaps he has done most justice to the facts where he has used his own imagination. In a wonderful way he has caught the atmosphere of the early church. He has given us not merely the facts, which were often of little moment, but the mood of the actors, the sense of mystery and power which overshadowed the young community. Christ had departed, but his place had now been taken by the Spirit, which was working mightily. It is from this point of view that Luke describes the life of the early church, and the impression which he leaves on us is far more real and convincing than if he had catalogued a great number of facts exactly as they happened.

The account in Acts is supplemented and illuminated by the Epistles of Paul. It is true that Paul wrote after the initial period had come to an end and the church had embarked on the great mission which in large measure changed its character. But again and again he has occasion to glance back on the preceding time, and his notices have a firsthand value which rarely can be claimed for those in the book of Acts. It must be remembered, too, that Paul had himself a close relation to the primitive community. Although he expressed his beliefs in new language they were in substance those of the earlier Apostles. Many of his modern critics, taking their cue unwittingly from the Jewish emissaries who tried to thwart his work, have described him as the adversary of the mother-church. This, as he strongly protested, was not true. He was the spokesman of the church, and when we ask ourselves what it claimed to be we receive the clearest answer from Paul.

Again, we learn much about the early community from the Synoptic Gospels. Their subject is the life of Jesus, but it was the church in Palestine which collected and preserved the records and threw them into their present form. It has been maintained by some scholars that the church was mainly responsible for the substance as well as the form, but this cannot be admitted for a moment. The sayings ascribed to Jesus are, for the most part, self-authenticating, and in many instances are at variance with the ideas of the church. Not only so, but almost always, as we shall see later, they are of such a character that no community could have devised them for its practical guidance. Here and there a strict command has been qualified, and in such cases we may suspect the hand of the church. But these modifications affect only a small part of the teaching and were evidently made when the initial period was over. It is not hard to distinguish the sayings which belong to the earliest stratum of the tradition, and which bear on them the stamp of Jesus' own mind.

We can thus gather from the Synoptic Gospels that the primitive community accepted the teaching of Jesus in its literal form. He had set up a standard which might seem impossible, but this was how he required his followers to live and they must make it their aim to obey him. The Christian rule as we know it in the Gospels was in very fact the rule of the primitive church. Above all, it accepted with a perfect confidence the promise of Jesus that the Kingdom of God would presently set in. This is the central theme of the Gospels. They tell how Jesus had proclaimed the Kingdom, how he had called on men to live for it, how he had suffered as the Messiah who was to bring it in. In the later New Testament writings the conception of the Kingdom tends to fall away. The precise meaning of it had apparently become obscure even in the time when the Gospels were finally put together. But in the minds of the earliest disciples there was no doubt. They knew that the message of Jesus had been that of the Kingdom of God; everything else had been subordinate to this one theme. It was on this message that the community took its stand.

For the understanding of the primitive church the Synoptic Gospels are thus of fundamental value. When Luke set himself to write its history in the book of Acts, he could find little to help him in the way of documents. The early church had been too much occupied with actual living to draw up records of what it had done and thought. But it had preserved the tradition of the message of Jesus, and this is also the self-revelation of the primitive church. For the purpose of its mission it had to tell the world what it believed, why it regarded Jesus as the Messiah, what was the way of life it was trying to follow. Although we had possessed no direct information about the early community we might have formed a picture of it, correct in all that matters, from the evidence of the Gospels alone.

It can hardly be emphasized too much that between the work of Jesus and the church that arose afterwards there was an intimate relation. Too often they have been kept separate, or have even been placed in opposition. Jesus, we are told, had lived and died, and after his death there grew up a community which called itself by his name but otherwise had little connection with him. Sometimes it has been argued that the creation of the church was the primary error which has darkened and nullified the whole meaning of the work of Jesus. He had looked for the Kingdom of God, the new age when men would be inwardly conformed to God's will. He had believed that in this coming time all outward authorities and systems would cease to be, for there would be no further need for them; they would only stand in the way of a real and immediate fellowship with God. But he had hardly departed when the Kingdom was forgotten and in place of it there appeared the church, which was only the old mechanical system over again. This has been singled out as the great apostasy of the Christian religion, which almost from the outset took a wrong direction and has been following it ever since. But the truth is that the church was bound up inseparably with Jesus' own work, and cannot otherwise be understood. This was recognized by Luke when he planned a history which should consist of two parts, integrally united. The first would tell of Jesus' life on earth; the second would describe the rise and expansion of his church. Both would have as their theme "the things which Jesus had done and said"[1]—only the one would deal with his life in the flesh, the other with his larger invisible life. This earliest of church historians had a clearer insight into the meaning of the church than any of his successors. They are content for the most part to examine the tree apart from the root. They tell us much of things that happened—successes, persecutions, formation of doctrines, modes of worship—but they have little light to throw on the inner forces which were at work through all the changes. The church is severed from the mission of Jesus himself, apart from which its own mission becomes meaningless.

It is part of the same error that the history of the church is usually treated as a development. In so far as a place is allowed

[1]Acts 1:1.

for Jesus, he is regarded as giving the initial impulse. Without him the church could never have begun, but his own achievement was relatively small. He was little more, perhaps, than a wandering Rabbi, inspired with wild apocalyptic hopes.[2] He worked for a brief period, two or three years at most, in a remote province of a tiny country, and left at his death a mere handful of disciples, all of them very ordinary men. His significance lies in the tremendous movement to which, by a series of amazing accidents, his work gave rise. The message which in natural course would have been soon forgotten was taken up by a succession of great thinkers, who developed it into a sublime religion, pregnant with high conceptions of which he himself was not more than dimly aware.

For this reading of the history Jesus was in some measure responsible. His parable of the grain of mustard-seed,[3] perverted from its true meaning, has determined almost all our thinking about the church. It is assumed that Jesus himself, hardly knowing what he did, planted a tiny seed, which grew in the course of centuries into a mighty tree which has overshadowed the earth. His parable falls in with our modern idea of evolution, which has proved so fruitful in many fields of knowledge that we apply it everywhere. We assume that in our religion as in all else there must have been a process of growth, a steady unfolding of the germ into ever richer fulfilment. In one sense, no doubt, this has happened. The church has grown enormously larger. Its institutions have been elaborated. The beliefs with which it started have given rise to vast theologies. But all this growth affects our religion only in its

[2]This view is adopted, rather surprisingly, by Otto in his book, *The Kingdom of God*.
[3]Matt. 13:31, 32.

external aspects and has not touched anything that belongs to its essence. The truth is that in things of the spirit the law of development does not apply. Homer is still one of the greatest of poets. There are works of early Egyptian sculpture which have never been surpassed. No later reflection on the mysteries of being has gone deeper than that of ancient India. It has often been noted that in work of a spiritual nature the height is sometimes reached at the beginning. There have been poets and artists who have never repeated what they could do in early youth. Nations have had their golden age in the very dawn of their history. Most of all in religion, the earliest phase, more often than not, is the great and decisive one. A revelation comes suddenly to some inspired prophet, and for ages afterwards his followers reflect on it, and expound it, and embody it in creeds and ceremonies; but it is never again apprehended as it was at the very start. The beginning is also the consummation.

In the study of Christianity, therefore, the theory of development can help us little, and tends only to distort the obvious facts. It requires us to think of Jesus as of little importance, except that he happened to give the initial impulse to a great movement. But he certainly did much more. He created the movement out of his own knowledge of God. None of those later thinkers who are supposed to have advanced on his message had anything essential to add to it. None of them, indeed, were able to comprehend it in anything like the fulness which it had for himself. This can be affirmed with certainty, for we possess the message as he gave it. From the later theologies men have always gone back to those words of Jesus, not merely because he spoke them, but because they are intrinsically greater than anything that came afterwards. As the writer of Hebrews says of him, he was at once the author and the perfecter of faith. It is absurd to speak of his teaching as nothing but the inconspicuous germ out of which the grandeur of Christian thought was finally to develop.

In like manner the primitive church is not to be regarded as a mere grain of mustard-seed; and by thus thinking of it we are blinded to its true significance. No doubt the comparison is just when we reckon by mass and number. The church of the day of Pentecost was assembled in one upper room, and it has since grown into a countless multitude: this expansion of the church has been the miracle of history. Yet on a deeper view there has been no development, for the church in its earliest days was actually more than it ever was to be afterwards. For that little time it answered to its true calling, and was never to rise again to the same level. All reformers in times since have made it their aim to restore the church to at least some semblance of what it was in the primitive days. They have erred, as we have seen, in their emphasis on mere accessories. It does not much matter how the early church was governed, how it selected and ordained its leaders, what forms it adopted in its sacraments or the conduct of its worship. In all such matters it was guided by custom or prudence or circumstance, and for similar reasons we are free to break away from its example. Yet the conception of the primitive church as the model for all later times is far more true to fact than the other view—that it was only a crude experiment, a sort of child's drawing of what a church might be. The true church existed in that primitive community. There has been no development from an imperfect, tentative phase into one of full maturity. For one brief period at the outset the fact, in some measure, corresponded to the ideal.

We cannot speak of a development of the church, and at the same time it is false to think of a deterioration. There never has been a time when Christian men have not complained that the church was declining—that it has grown weak in faith, loose in doctrine, careless in moral standards. More especially in the older Protestantism the study of church history was dominated by the idea of a corruption that had set in after the close of the first century. Until that time the church had been pure. It had been free from all division, intent on its high vocation, firm in its loyalty to the genuine Christian teaching. Then, for various reasons, there had been a falling away. The original Apostles were now dead, and their successors were ignorant and weak. Gentiles had poured into the church, bringing with them their pagan beliefs and practices. Worst of all, a worldly spirit had begun to assert itself. Christians were no longer single-hearted in the cause, but were ambitious and self-seeking, and the church was turned into a half-secular society. Now it cannot be doubted that in this view there was a measure of truth. Even towards the end of the second century earnest men were beginning to feel that something had gone wrong. The Montanist movement, with all its extravagances, won a large following because it offered a necessary protest against the abuses which for many years had been creeping into the church.

Nevertheless, the old theory of a corruption which suddenly began after the New Testament period may now be thrown aside. It can be refuted, for that part, from the New Testament itself. The communities to which Paul wrote his letters were by no means examples of a pure Christianity. Paul has occasion to rebuke jealousies, divisions, even immoralities "such as are not named among the Gentiles."[4] The average standard of conduct in the later church was probably a good deal higher than in the first century. Moral education is always a slow process, and after two or three generations of Christian training a level was reached which was not attainable among converts who had come straight from heathenism. Much the same may be said of belief and doctrine. In the early mission it was difficult to impress the Christian ideas on minds to which they were entirely strange. Paul finds himself obliged to speak, in every Epistle, of lapses into Judaism or pagan speculation. In all the later New Testament books we hear of "false teachings" which had become a grave danger. Those early heresies, too, did not turn, like most of the later ones, on subtle differences of doctrine, but on strange beliefs which struck at the central principles of the Christian faith. It is thus historically false to think of the New Testament church as pure and the later one as subject to a growing corruption. Judging by ordinary standards there was rather a constant improvement. To Christians of the later generations the higher principles, in which they had been nurtured from childhood, were a second nature, and in the fires of persecution which now broke out at intervals the baser elements in the church were burned out. There may have been few conspicuous saints, but the average quality of Christian faith and living was always growing higher.

A change was indeed taking place, of which all thoughtful

[4]I Cor. 5:1.

Christians were keenly aware, but it cannot be properly described as a corruption. Its nature is best indicated in the Epistle to the Hebrews, where the writer deplores the indifference which had come over the church of his generation. It had lost the primitive ardour, the sense of something new and wonderful, the confidence that in Christianity God had given His final revelation. This change, as the writer himself recognizes, was partly due to mere lapse of time.[5] The first enthusiasm had now died down, as it was certain to do. Those who were born into the Christian faith were unable to prize it like the original converts, who had discovered it for themselves. But there were two special causes which had led to the indifference, and it is well to note them, for they have a close bearing on the whole problem of the early church.

On the one hand, the first disciples had looked for the immediate return of Christ to establish his Kingdom on earth. It was on this hope that the church had based itself, and now, to all appearance, it had proved illusory. The writer of Hebrews assures his readers that it still holds good. Years have gone by, but "yet a little while, and the Coming One will come and will not tarry."[6] It was difficult, however, to restore the old vitality to this hope, and the Christian attitude towards it was becoming ever more doubtful. Since the Lord had not yet come, would he ever come? Deeply religious natures were able, like the Fourth Evangelist, to understand the Coming in a spiritual sense and to perceive that Christ had already returned, as an inward presence, to those that loved him. But for ordinary Christians the hope had largely lost its meaning. From habit and training they remained in the church. They

[5]Heb. 5:12; 6:10 f.; 10:32.   [6]Heb. 10:37.

accepted its doctrines, and valued its moral guidance. But their religion was growing cold and perfunctory, since it was no longer quickened by the glorious hope which had inspired the early disciples.

There was another cause, closely related to this one, which acted still more powerfully in changing the character of the church. Since the Lord had not appeared and the Kingdom was not to come in immediately, it was evident that Christians must resign themselves to a continuance of the present age. They had believed at first that this world might be disregarded. It was so near its end that they could hold aloof from it and submit themselves without reserve to that higher law which would prevail in the future. Now it was recognized that this could not be. The existing conditions were to last on, and the Christian, like other men, must conform to them. He must mix with his neighbours and defer to their customs and prejudices. He was involved in a social system which had claims on him, and while holding to his religion he must bring it into some kind of harmony with the earthly life. There were always Christians to whom any concession to this world seemed to be like a betrayal. The writer of Hebrews belonged, apparently, to this Puritan type, and is anxious that the primitive code should still be observed in all its strictness. He declares that after the great renewal by which a man becomes a Christian no second repentance is possible; those who fall away will be irretrievably doomed.[7]

The church at large, however, accepted the fact that it was still in this world, and must allow for human weakness and limitations. As a consequence it ceased to insist on the absolute

[7]Heb. 6:4 f.

Christian rule, and many of its members, at least in the eyes of a rigorous judge, became lukewarm or quite indifferent. But the change was not in any sense a "corruption." Rightly considered, it was inevitable when once the church had begun to realize that it had to continue side by side with the world. We have to think not of a perversion but of an adjustment. After the failure of the original hope the church found itself in a new position, and had to choose one of two alternatives. Either it had to withdraw entirely from the world, or it had to adapt itself as best it could to the world's conditions, which were plainly destined to endure. It chose the second course. Maintaining itself as the community of the Kingdom it sought to make its home in the existing world, and it has pursued this effort for nearly two thousand years.

There is thus a twofold significance in the history of the early church. It reveals to us, on the one hand, what the church was, in its original conception, and must always essentially be. The first disciples looked for the Kingdom which Christ was presently to bring in at his glorious coming. They were the heirs of the Kingdom, which was so close at hand that they could live for it as if it were already here. The present world had ceased to exist for them; they belonged wholly to the world which was to come. On the other hand, we learn from that early history how the church gradually changed its character. It realized that the world was to continue, and that the new community must somehow fit itself into the given framework. Jesus had taught how men were to live in the Kingdom; could not his message be so applied and interpreted that they might live by it on this earth? The church was the community of the Kingdom, and it never ceased to be so; but it sought to be faithful to its high calling and at the same time to acclimatize itself in the present world.

This in all times has been the problem which has confronted the church. It stands for ideals and interests which cannot be realized by earthly beings, and the endeavour to live by them in their full extent is found invariably to defeat itself. Ever and again communities have arisen which have aimed at a perfect compliance with all the precepts of Jesus. They have forbidden any resentment of injuries, any personal desires or possessions. Societies of this kind have always made shipwreck, in a very short time, on the hard facts of the actual world. Individual Christians have set themselves from time to time to follow out literally the teaching of the Gospels, and we owe them an infinite debt. The meaning of Christianity would be quickly forgotten unless there were at least a few in every generation who have sought to bring home to us what the Christian life ultimately involves. Yet this complete obedience has always ended in some kind of disaster. No story is more tragic than that of the aged Tolstoi, broken in health and spirit, alienated from his family and friends, disappointed in all his hopes, dying miserably at last by the roadside—all because he had tried without reserve to follow the way of life which seemed to be enjoined on him by the Gospels. We are familiar in our time with the watchword "Back to Christ." It is continually impressed on us that if Christianity is ever again to become a living power we must throw aside all later interpretations and act, with perfect simplicity, on Jesus' own teaching.

"Christianity," according to Lessing's oft-quoted saying,

"has been practised for eighteen centuries, but the religion of Jesus has never been tried." This is true, and there is a reason for it, but it is not to be found in the perversity of theologians or the blindness and selfishness of the church. The religion of Jesus has never been put into action because it cannot be. It makes demands on us which, in the last resort, are incapable of fulfilment under the given conditions of this world.

Jesus himself was fully aware of the impracticable nature of his message. He admitted that "with man this is impossible" —in the present age the perfect will of God cannot be fulfilled; and this, as he clearly saw, was not due simply to the evil consequences of human greed and folly. Modern reformers are confident that if only we had some new economic system, if the opportunities for a good life were freely open to everybody, all the obstacles to a true Christian society would soon be removed. But Jesus himself was under no such delusion. He perceived that this world, however we may improve it, will still be the world. It is so constituted that so long as it endures men will be debarred from the higher life. A time will indeed come when the poor, the meek, the merciful, the sorrowing will be blessed; but the world, as we now know it, is plainly for the strong, the self-confident, the aggressive. Plants and animals thrive in their own climate, and the man who prospers in this world must always be the worldly man. Jesus pronounced his beatitudes on those who were looking for a different world. When it comes they in their turn will find happiness, but not till then.

We have here the great paradox of Christianity. It answers, like no other religion, to that law which, as Paul says, is written in the hearts of all men.[8] With our deepest instincts we know that its demands are right, and that love, truth, goodness, fidelity have an absolute claim upon us. Yet by all earthly standards the gospel, as Paul again acknowledges, is foolishness.[9] It runs counter to all maxims of prudence, to all those courses of action which the world stamps with its approval by its rewards of wealth, success, reputation, happiness. We have here a contradiction which was brought, as it were, to a burning focus in the Cross of Christ. By all worldly modes of judgment the Cross was the supreme folly. Jesus had himself to blame for the disaster. He had paid no heed to public opinion; he had aroused powerful enemies quite needlessly; he had taken no thought for his personal safety; he had wilfully thrown away the happiness that was within his reach and had aimed at the impossible. His death on the Cross, before his days were half over, might well be taken as an awful warning of how men ought not to live, and doubtless it was so used at the time by many respected teachers. From their own point of view they were right. If a man desires that all should go well with him he must exercise ordinary wisdom. Jesus had defied the principles on which this world is built, and he deserved his death, like a man who rushes blindly into a stream of traffic, or lives contrary to all the rules of health. Yet the Cross has appealed to all men since as the very symbol of all that is highest and most glorious in human life. Jesus was utterly wrong by all the world's standards; why do we have that certainty that he was divinely right?

Only one explanation is possible. Belonging to this world we must submit to its order, but we are conscious of another

[8] Rom. 2:15.   [9] I Cor. 1:23, 24.

world to which we also belong. It has an order of its own, different from the earthly one and most often opposed to it. In his ultimate nature man is a being of that other world, and in obeying its law he realizes his true life. Jesus called on men to live for the higher order. His disciples took up his teaching and sought to put it into effect, and for this purpose they formed the church as a brotherhood in which the new law of living should take the place of the old. But they presently found themselves confronted with an insuperable difficulty. What they had received from Jesus was the law of the higher and future order, and they were bound in by the present one, which is subject to a different law.

It is one of the commonplaces of modern religious teaching that Christianity is a very simple thing, which has been needlessly complicated by doctrine and ritual. Nothing is required of any one who would be truly Christian but to act consistently according to the rules laid down in the Sermon on the Mount. It is assumed that when Christianity is thus understood all the difficulties fall away, and it becomes a practical religion, within the reach of any high-minded man. This, however, is a profound error. If Christianity means obedience to the Sermon on the Mount, no one can ever hope to be a Christian. Not even the best of men could undertake to fulfil a single one of those precepts of Jesus for an hour together. To be absolutely pure and unselfish and sincere; to love one's enemies and forgive without limit; to have no care for tomorrow and trust everything to God; this is indeed Christianity, but who can attain to it? Men have sought to be Christians in many strange and difficult ways. They have remained for years on the top of lofty pillars; they have stood waist-deep the whole day in icy water, reciting prayers; they have forced themselves to believe every article of the most preposterous creeds. All this is easy, compared to a full obedience to the precepts of the Sermon on the Mount.

The law of Christ is manifestly impracticable. It requires that in this world, with our limited capacity as earthly beings, we should live by a rule which cannot be carried out except in a different order of things. The primitive church had thus a problem before it which it attempted to solve. Jesus had called on his disciples to live as in the Kingdom, and in answer to his call the church arose. But it found itself still involved in the earthly order, and its task henceforth was to reconcile the two loyalties. How could it be true to its vocation as the church of Christ, and yet adapt itself to the earthly conditions under which it must exist? In two ways, therefore, the study of the primitive church is of surpassing value. It enables us, on the one hand, to understand the church as it was at the outset, when it took its commission directly from the hands of Jesus. In the light of its beginnings we can perceive the intrinsic nature of the church. On the other hand, we see how the church entered on its task of integrating itself with the present world. The methods which it then devised have proved themselves, by the experience of many centuries, to be the most effective. Our task today is the same as it was then, and in all efforts to accomplish it we find our best guidance in the history of those first days.

CHAPTER II

THE CHURCH AND THE MESSAGE OF JESUS

From the beginning the church called itself by the name of Christ. It was made up of his disciples, and continued his work after his departure. Admission to it was by a rite of baptism in which he was acknowledged as "the Lord." That in some way it owed its existence to him cannot be doubted, and he has commonly been regarded as founding it by his deliberate act.

This belief might seem to be confirmed by the explicit evidence of the famous text, now inscribed in letters of gold over the shrine of St. Peter at Rome. "Thou art Peter, and on this rock I will build my church, and the gates of hell shall not prevail against it." This verse, however, is open to grave question. The passage of which it forms a part (Matt. 16:16–19) may well go back to some authentic utterance of Jesus, for the imagery is strongly Hebraic, and is fully in the manner of his other sayings. Matthew, whose gifts are merely those of a skilful compiler, could not himself have invented an utterance so bold and splendid and characteristic. As it stands, however, it is more than suspicious. Mark, on whom Matthew is dependent throughout the chapter, knows nothing of this addition, and it is quite out of keeping with the incident to which it is attached. Peter had earned no special privilege by his confession, for he had only acted as spokesman for the whole band of disciples. Nor can Jesus have been in the mood to congratulate and reward him, for he was accepting the Messiahship as a terrible burden from which there was no escape.

Apart from this passage there is no indication that Jesus ever contemplated the church in its historical form. One fact alone is sufficient proof that he was not consciously its Founder. When it entered on its career after his death it was obliged at every step to feel its own way, with many misgivings. Differences were constantly arising with regard to government, institutions, forms of worship, and they have continued ever since, with lamentable results to the harmony of the church. If Jesus had foreseen and planned a new community he would have prescribed at least a few simple rules for its guidance, as all religious founders have been careful to do. Apparently he made no such provision. The leaders who followed him were never able to settle any of their controversies on matters of church order by direct appeal to Jesus' own authority. He had often spoken of forgiveness, kindness, helpfulness, willingness to take the lower place. These general sayings with regard to social duties and relations were scrupulously preserved, and now and then they are so applied in our Gospels as to make them serve as rules for the Christian brotherhood. But nothing of a more specific nature could be found in his teaching. He had dealt with broad human relations, and had never, apparently, concerned himself with that particular society which was to take form in the church.

In the strict sense, therefore, Jesus was not the Founder of the church. It may plausibly be argued that a formal organization, with regular officials and stated ordinances, was contrary to his whole intention. He had looked for a time when no external bond would be necessary, and men would serve

God freely and spontaneously because they were in inward sympathy with His will. Nevertheless, the church was the direct outcome of the work of Jesus. This is evident, if from nothing else, from the fact that it had no formal beginning. Luke is aware of the tremendous importance of the new departure, and is anxious to find some definite occasion when the church began. He fixes on the day of Pentecost, with its wonderful manifestations; but whatever happened on that day it is apparent, from Luke's own narrative, that the church was already in being. Its members were actually in session as a church when they received the gift of the Spirit. There was no set day when the church was born. The disciples did not convene a solemn meeting and resolve, after full deliberation, that they would form themselves into a Christian society. They simply continued to live together, as they had done in Jesus' lifetime, and without their knowing the church came to be.

The view has been put forward in recent years,[1] and there is much to be said for it, that the ordinance of the Lord's Supper had a twofold root. It commemorated the Supper which Jesus had held with his disciples on the eve of his death, but this had been only the last of many similar meals which were well remembered. Jesus had been accustomed to close the day with a simple repast, at which he conversed freely with his companions; and it was on these occasions, more than on any others, that they had come near to him and learned to know him. In after days they associated him most vividly with these common meals. This would seem to be the suggestion in the

[1]It is admirably presented by A. B. Macdonald in his book *Christian Worship in the Primitive Church*.

story of the journey to Emmaus, when the two disciples failed to recognize their fellow-traveller until they began a meal with him and "knew him as he distributed the bread."[2] These words can have no reference to the Last Supper, for the two disciples are described as outside the circle of the Twelve. But all who were on terms of friendship with Jesus were familiar with his characteristic actions at the evening meals at which they had sometimes been present.

After his death it was only natural that his followers should maintain the practice of a common supper, and this is expressly mentioned in a significant notice in the book of Acts: "They continued in the fellowship and in the breaking of bread."[3] Jesus was no longer with them, but they could not take part in the accustomed meal without remembering how he had formerly presided at it. They believed that he was still invisibly present, and with the ordinary meal they combined a brief ceremony re-enacting what he had done and said at the Last Supper. In this theory there is much that is attractive, and it offers a natural explanation of how the Supper came to be adopted as a standing ordinance. In a manner it already bore this character. The disciples merely perpetuated the custom which Jesus had taught them, and around this custom the Christian society grew.

So when it is affirmed that Jesus himself was the Founder of the church, a fact of supreme importance is stated in the wrong way. He did not deliberately plan this new society but it originated with him, not merely because he gave the impulse which led to its formation but in a more definite way. It consisted, at the outset, of his personal followers, who aimed

[2]Luke 24:31.   [3]Acts 2:42.

at continuing after he was gone the life which they had known in his company. They believed in his promises; they sought to obey his precepts; they maintained the brotherly relation into which he had brought them; they perpetuated his custom of a common meal, and thought of him as still presiding. There was no break with their previous life, no new beginning. The church was simply the group of Jesus' followers, seeking to continue as they had been before. Their numbers grew, but they went on observing the fellowship which had begun under Jesus' direction, and in this manner the church arose. For some time it had no formal organization. Everything was left to the control of the Spirit, which had now taken possession of the community and was believed in some way to represent Jesus himself. Thus no line can be drawn between the company of disciples which Jesus had formed in his lifetime and the church that came into being after his death. It was the same community, expanding and shaping itself, and it had originated with Jesus himself.

Since the church thus arose unconsciously, of its own accord, there is no need to seek its origin in suggestions from the outside. It has been assumed often that Christianity simply took over the Old Testament conception of Israel, the chosen people of God, with the one difference that faith instead of race was made the bond of union. A view of this kind might seem to be adopted in the New Testament itself, and this is not surprising. The disciples were Jews, and knew of no other type of religious association than the Jewish community. They believed that God had made his promises to Abraham and would fulfil his purpose with the world through Abraham's seed. They took for granted, therefore, that the church was Israel, or at least the faithful remnant which in the sight of God, as the prophets had declared, was the true Israel. It is pointed out that the name which the church adopted, apparently from the outset, was "the Ecclesia," a name applied in scripture to the congregation of Israel. Paul in one place[4] speaks explicitly of "the Israel of God," and in the speech of Stephen, perhaps the earliest Christian document which has come down to us, the whole argument turns on the idea that Israel as a nation has been rejected and has surrendered its privileges to the true Israel, the church.

Now it cannot be denied that the Old Testament conception had far-reaching effects on Christian thought. Almost as soon as the church became fully conscious of itself it took the ancient community as its model and sought to bring its own ordinances into line with it. Jewish thinkers, especially in the Dispersion, had already given a spiritual interpretation to the old ritual, and it was not difficult to prove by this method that the church had its temple, its sacrifices, its rite of circumcision, its law and covenant. In all respects it was the Israel of the past, brought at length to its consummation. This line of thought is elaborately worked out in the Epistle to the Hebrews. Yet it is wrong to conceive of the church as breaking away from the old Israel in order to form a new one, similar in character but renovated and purified. So far from regarding itself as a substitute for Israel, its chief anxiety at the outset was to be recognized as a legitimate Jewish sect. So far from trying to repeat the ancient customs it laid all the stress on what was distinctive in its own worship and beliefs and mode of life.

[4]Gal. 6: 16.

It was the "new Israel" in the sense that while it remained part of Israel it was altogether new. Something different had emerged from the old conception of a chosen people.

The truth is that even if the Jewish community had never existed, the church, in all its essential features, was bound to result from the mission of Jesus. Those who believed in him felt themselves to be brethren, and in the effort to follow out his teaching could not but form a new society. As Jews they borrowed much from the example of Israel, but the wonder is that it affected them so little. Instead of copying the Jewish institutions they adopted new ones, springing out of the inherent nature of their new faith. Nothing is more remarkable than this independence which is everywhere manifest in the life of the early church. Perhaps it was due in some measure to the very fact that the disciples continued to be Jews, practising the old religion along with their own. They did not need to devise some equivalent for the Law and the priesthood and the ritual, for in their Jewish faith they had all these things already. Their whole mind was devoted to the discovery of what was required of them by their new beliefs, and they were able to build up the church with a splendid freedom. It was not the Jewish community over again, with a few minor differences, but was a new creation.

The roots of the church are thus to be sought in the Christian message itself, and to determine what the church was we have to consider the nature of that message. Within a generation it came to involve a number of new elements and was formulated by Paul in theological terms. Even when it was thus elaborated it depended for its meaning on one central belief, and this, at the outset, included everything. Jesus had declared that the Kingdom of God was at hand. All his teaching is concerned with this message, and his death also has to be understood in the light of it. The "gospel," as we now employ the term, has a wide variety of meanings, but for Jesus himself it was simply the "good tidings" that the Kingdom, so long expected, was now on the way. The church arose out of this gospel. In the last resort it was nothing but the message of Jesus, expressed in a concrete form.

Jesus never defined the Kingdom of God, partly, no doubt, because he could take for granted that his hearers all knew in a general manner what it signified. Ever since the days of the prophets the hope of Israel had been directed to a future time when God, who was now acknowledged only by His chosen people, would assert His sovereignty over the whole world. The prophets had looked forward to this future age, expecting that God would bring it in through forces that were already operative in human history. But in the century before Christ the hope had taken another direction. It now seemed apparent that in the present world evil had proved triumphant. Israel had been worsted in the struggle with earthly powers. Society was growing more corrupt and contained in it no elements which could possibly make for a better day. If God were to establish His Kingdom He must destroy the present order entirely and replace it with a new one. There can be little doubt that Jesus attached himself to this hope, which pervades the Jewish apocalyptic writings.[5] He took up the message of John

[5]It has been argued very ably by F. C. Grant (*The Gospel of the Kingdom*) that Jesus was little affected by apocalyptic ideas of the Kingdom. This view, however, involves an arbitrary treatment of the Gospel sources.

the Baptist that the Kingdom was at hand, and his message, at least superficially, was similar to that of John. A time of crisis was near in which the whole existing order would be dissolved, and God, by His own immediate act or through His agent the Messiah, would inaugurate the new age.

In one respect, however, the conception of Jesus was different from that of John and the apocalyptic thinkers. Apocalyptic had laid all the stress on the outward attributes of the Kingdom. The earth was to be ten times more fruitful; Israel was to overcome all enemies; pain and danger would disappear; heaven and earth would draw together, and men would be raised to the status of angels. Jesus may have accepted these beliefs, but he hardly touches on them in the whole course of his teaching, and they must have meant little to him. He speaks many parables to explain what the Kingdom would be like, but he never employs that sensuous imagery in which all the apocalyptic writers delight and which is familiar to us from the book of Revelation. His one interest is in the spiritual conditions which will prevail in the new age. Men will have the true knowledge of God; they will obey him gladly and spontaneously; they will be bound in loving service to each other; their aims and motives will be completely different from what they are now. All that belongs to the mere setting of the great future falls into the background; the one thing that matters is the new relation to God, the perfect obedience to His will. For apocalyptic thought the future world is essentially the present one, raised to a higher power, renewed and glorified, but intrinsically the same. Jesus thinks of a world which will be different in kind. The present order of things will give place to another.

It may be questioned indeed whether our modern knowledge of apocalyptic, which is supposed to have thrown a brilliant new light on the thought of Jesus, has not tended rather to obscure it. For the last half century all investigation of the Gospels has turned on the fresh data supplied by the apocalyptic writings. It is assumed that now, with the aid of these long-lost documents, we are in a position to define the real ideas which lay behind Jesus' teaching. We have learned to see that he was one in a succession of Jewish thinkers who were occupied with speculations about the future. His message of the Kingdom of God may be correlated with various passages in the apocalyptic books, and may thus be restored to its authentic meaning. This, however, is to leave out of account the one thing which is vital. By means of what he borrows from apocalyptic Jesus is seeking to express a great conception of his own. It had come to him, not from previous teachers, but by immediate vision; and all that really matters is this significance which the Kingdom had for Jesus himself. To use a very inadequate illustration, it has been proved that when Wordsworth wrote his glorious poem "Tintern Abbey," he had been reading Hartley, a minor philosopher of the eighteenth century, and had been impressed by some of his theories. A critical student of the poem would undoubtedly need to acquaint himself with the work of this forgotten thinker, but it was certainly not from him that the poet had learned to look on nature with "a sense of something far more deeply interfused." There may be ideas and phrases in the poem which can be better elucidated when we have studied the philosophy, but it owes all its splendour and passion to an intense experience which was the poet's own. So we come little nearer to an understanding of Jesus by a knowledge of his apocalyptic background. We run the danger, rather, of mistaking for his real intention what was nothing but its accidental wrapping. He proclaimed the Kingdom as he had himself known it, and as he would have known it although there had been no apocalyptic tradition. He might have expressed himself in different terms, but the substance of his thought would have been the same.

What did he mean, then, by the Kingdom of God, which he describes under those apocalyptic forms which were provided for him by the Jewish thinking of his time? Clearly he has in his mind something which is the highest conceivable good. The Fourth Evangelist does not employ the term "Kingdom of God," but represents Jesus as speaking always of "eternal life," and in some Synoptic passages Jesus himself identifies the Kingdom with life, carried to its perfection in a higher world. His idea is difficult and elusive because it is so comprehensive. In each period of Christian history it has taken on a new meaning, and has been understood as the communion of saints, the future blessedness, the inward fellowship with God, the moral law, the final brotherhood of man. Different as they are, these interpretations are all involved in the thought of Jesus, although each of them by itself is one-sided. They need to be blended together, and even in their sum total they are inadequate, for in Jesus' own mind they are only facets of a larger conception which includes and transcends them.

He was seeking, in fact, to express by the language of Jewish apocalyptic the truth which is fundamental in all religion. Men have always been conscious that over against the visible world there is another, which is the real one. Apart from this conviction man's life has no sense or value; the purposes which he knows in his heart to be the highest all fall to the ground. Religion in its ultimate meaning is nothing but this assurance of a higher, spiritual world. Jesus possessed it in a supreme degree. Living on earth he was continually aware of that higher order for which all things exist. We feel as we listen to his words that he is seeing through all veils to the divine reality. He lives wholly for that higher order which he calls the Kingdom of God.

It has often been disputed whether he thought of the Kingdom as in the future or as already begun. In a number of passages he seems to use the language of the present. He points to the works done by him as evidence that the Kingdom has come. He speaks of John the Baptist as closing an age which has now given place to another. He compares the Kingdom to seed which is already in the ground, although it has still to spring up and grow. The view has been held by some recent scholars that he conceived of his ministry as the actual beginning of the great final drama. Prophets and apocalyptists had looked for a day when God would interpose in human history and establish a new order. Jesus was aware that with him this higher dispensation had begun; and ever since although men have failed to perceive it they have been living under its control.

The theory is an impressive one,[6] but on closer examination it breaks down. For one thing, in spite of sayings that might appear to point the other way, the main emphasis of the

[6]Its best exponent is C. H. Dodd, in his books, *The Parables of the Kingdom* and *The Apostolic Message*.

gospel teaching is on the idea of futurity. The Kingdom is a glorious hope which sustains men in their earthly struggle and offers them a goal towards which they can strive. "Thy Kingdom come" is the central petition of the Lord's Prayer and is meant to define the abiding mood of the Christian life. Jesus was himself supported by this hope of the future Kingdom, and by means of it he seems to have explained to himself the purpose of his death. "I have a baptism to be baptized with, and how am I straitened till it be accomplished."[7] The work appointed to him was the bringing in of the Kingdom, and as yet he could not achieve it. Although the Kingdom was at hand there was some tremendous obstacle which stood in the way of its coming, and till this was removed he could effect nothing. How he conceived of this obstacle we have no means of knowing, and perhaps he never tried to define it, as Paul was to do afterwards. Yet he believed, when he saw his death to be inevitable, that in this way only could the barrier be thrown down. He had proclaimed the Kingdom and prepared men for entering it, but God had so willed that it could not be realized except through his death. This is the train of thought which seems to underlie the account of the Last Supper.

It may be gathered from the whole attitude of the early church that Jesus had described the Kingdom as future. The disciples were acquainted with his mind as we, who know it only through the few sayings preserved to us, cannot pretend to be. They were aware that he had looked forward to a great coming manifestation, and now they eagerly awaited it. The Lord had died and risen again and had thus attained to his

[7]Luke 12:50.

full office as Messiah. Everything was now ready. At any moment he might return from heaven, and the Kingdom which he had promised would become a fact. The mood of the early church is inexplicable unless we can assume that Jesus, by the whole tenor of his teaching, had inspired the disciples with a mighty hope. In the midst of seeming disaster they were able to wait with confidence for the fulfilment which was presently to come.

There is thus little historical basis for the theory that Jesus thought of the Kingdom as now realized; and its religious value is doubtful. As Paul says, when he declares that the Christian salvation is still future, "Hope that is seen is not hope, but if we hope for what we see not, then do we with patience wait for it."[8] His meaning is that hope loses its quality and its moral power when its object is assured. The Christian message must point forward to something not yet attained if it is to bring strength and endurance. In the Middle Ages the idea of the Kingdom as present succeeded for a time in capturing the Christian mind. The church was regarded as itself the Kingdom; whatever the church decreed was to be accepted without question as the final will of God. As a result of this mode of thinking religion was in danger of extinction. It was saved only by the enduring confidence that over against the church on earth there was the church invisible. The true consummation was still in the realm of hope.

For Jesus, therefore, as for the prophets and the apocalyptic teachers, the Kingdom lay in the future. If he seems at times to conceive of it as present this is only because it is so real to him that the brief period before its coming passes almost out

[8]Rom. 8:24, 25.

of sight. Here, it is sometimes held, he fell into a delusion which vitiated his message at its very centre. Not only did he work with apocalyptic ideas which have now lost their meaning, but he expected in the immediate future a fulfilment of which there is still no sign after all these ages. What can be the worth of a religion which was thus based on a. palpable error? Now it may be granted that Jesus speaks, in the apocalyptic manner, of a coming age, and imagines it as near at hand. In this he was mistaken, but the mistake was due to nothing else than the clearness and certainty of his vision. The Kingdom was for him so real that he thought of it, not as a vague possibility or an object in the far distance, but as almost near enough to touch. When he says that it is at hand he only expresses his vivid sense of its reality. More than once, for that part, he disclaims any exact knowledge of times and seasons; all this he leaves in the hand of God. What he is sure of is the fact of a higher order, different from that which we know. In the Kingdom the laws of this world are reversed; all aims and desires and ways of living take a new direction; the will of God is perfectly fulfilled.

At a later time Christian thinkers, as they reflected on the message of Jesus, broke away from the apocalyptic scheme. They conceived, not of two ages but of two worlds, over against each other. For Paul and John and the writer to the Hebrews men can seek even now to rise out of the lower world into the higher. Jesus did not state his thought in this manner. He adhered, at least in form, to the apocalyptic tradition, and declared that God was shortly to destroy the present order and establish another in its place. But while he expressed himself in terms of time, his mind was set, as the later writers per-

The Nature of the Early Church

ceived, on the two opposing worlds. As men are now they cannot apprehend the Kingdom. Something conceals it from them, and the veil may be represented as one of time. Jesus was content to think of it in this manner, and declared that a day was coming when the Kingdom would be made manifest. But his real interest is in the contrast between the higher world and this visible one. Men have accepted the present order and conformed their lives to it, but there is another order of things in which the earthly standards and values cease to have meaning. As children of God men belong to this higher world. They must set their hearts on it and reach forward to it; they must undergo a change of mind so as to live henceforth according to its law. The apocalyptic setting does not affect the real thought of Jesus. When he declared that a crisis was at hand in which this world would come to an end and give place to the Kingdom, he meant, essentially, that the other order was entirely different from this one. All that now appears most certain must be counted as an illusion if we are to follow the true will of God. The teaching of Jesus would have been much the same even if he had known that the Kingdom, which he believed near at hand, would not come for ages. He never expected that it could be realized under earthly conditions. The present order must first come to an end, and it made little difference whether this happened tomorrow or after the lapse of thousands of years. Men could believe in it and set their minds on it and do God's will on earth as it is done in heaven. In this sense, that it might be apprehended as a present reality, the Kingdom was near.

Jesus thus conceived of the Kingdom as the higher order, entirely separate from that of the world we know. It cannot, therefore, proceed from this world but must come supernaturally. The view is often put forward in our day, as almost self-evident, that for the apocalyptic ideas employed by Jesus we must now substitute those of evolution. He looked for a tremendous change, and expected, in accordance with the thought of his time, that it would come suddenly and supernaturally. We have now learned that the great changes are not effected in this manner. The Kingdom is not to come in a moment, but, like everything else, must grow. It will come in, not by way of sudden miracle but gradually, through the silent, continued action of Christian men and women. They are helping it steadily forward by the creation of a better society, by increase of knowledge and mastery of material forces, by the constant amelioration of laws and morals. All this, however, is quite alien to the thought of Jesus—not because he lived in an unenlightened age, but because he drew a clear distinction between the earthly and the divine order. Man cannot bring in the Kingdom any more than he can control the tides and the seasons. It is God's Kingdom and man can do nothing but wait for its coming and prepare himself to receive it. So when Jesus describes it in apocalyptic fashion as appearing unexpectedly and all in a moment, he only uses the traditional language to express a cardinal element in his own conception. God will manifest His Kingdom by a divine act without any co-operation on the part of men. Yet He cannot so manifest it until men are earnestly seeking it, and to this extent they can help Him. They are to pray for the Kingdom; they are to repent and follow the new righteousness. God offers the Kingdom, and by seeking to do His will they respond to Him and prevail on Him to hasten His purpose. They can anticipate the Kingdom by trying to live even now as if it were come.

Theory of an interim ethic

It has been pointed out by acute scholars in recent years that the teaching of Jesus involves a contradiction. He conceives of the Kingdom as still in the future, and as altogether different from anything we can yet know; but in all his sayings he presupposes the present conditions. He bids men be kind and just and merciful, although in the Kingdom there will be no suffering, no oppression, no weakness or poverty. He insists on the duty of forgiveness, but in the Kingdom there will be nothing to forgive, since no one will wrong his neighbour. He bids us trust in God, even when he seems forgetful, but in the Kingdom, when all will know God as the Father, it will be impossible to doubt Him. The Gospel ethic, it may be fairly argued, will all become meaningless as soon as the Kingdom arrives. It has reference not to the new conditions under which men will live hereafter, but to the present earthly conditions which will have passed away. The view has therefore been held that Jesus meant his teaching to have only an "interim" value. He thought of the Kingdom as coming soon, but not immediately. There would be a period of waiting, and his followers required to know how they should act in this brief but critical interval. No one can yet imagine anything as to the nature of life in the Kingdom. The relations of men to each other will be totally different from what they are now, and Jesus did not presume to lay down rules for that mysterious future. All that he offered was an interim ethic, which indeed made strenuous demands, for in view of the approaching Judgment the standards cannot be pitched too high. Yet the situation which he keeps before him is that of the existing order. According as men discharge their duty in it they will earn the right to enter the Kingdom.

This theory is based on the false conception that what Jesus gave was a number of set rules, which were to be literally obeyed. It is clear, however, when we examine his teaching more closely, that he was concerned not with rules but with principles. The various sayings and parables are intended merely as illustrations of how those principles should be applied. For this purpose he takes his examples from life as it is now, for he could not do otherwise. But the circumstances make no difference to the principles themselves. When the Kingdom comes, love and mercy will find expression in ways which we cannot yet imagine, but in essence they will be the same as they are now. The man who performs an act of kindness is doing God's will as it will be done in the Kingdom. His act, no doubt, is determined by conditions which will one day cease to be. He may be a Samaritan who takes pity on a wounded traveller whom others have passed by, and in the Kingdom of God there will be no robbers who leave men bleeding by the roadside and no selfish priests and levites. But kindness, however it is manifested, has the divine quality. It conforms to the will of God as it must always be.

But the theory of an interim ethic lies open to another and more serious criticism. Jesus cannot have meant his teaching to have only a provisional value, for it could never be put into action, even for the shortest interval. It differs from every other type of ethic precisely in this, that it always insists on the absolute standard. Love must be all-inclusive; forgiveness must have no limit; goodness must be unalloyed, like that of God.

An ethic of this kind is altogether beyond man's reach. In order to follow it man's whole nature and the world he lives in would need to be transformed. The idea that Jesus had nothing in mind but the moral requirements of a few months or years involves an utter misunderstanding. Instead of concentrating on the short time which has still to run, he disregards it altogether. He looks beyond this world to the higher one. The old commandments, as he expressly points out, were meant for the existing state of things. They made concessions to "the hardness of men's hearts," to the earthly hindrances and restrictions to which man's life is subject. A day is coming when all the conditions, inward and outward, will be changed, and Jesus is intent on showing what life will then be. It is not his purpose simply to raise the current morality, so that men may be better prepared for the approaching Judgment. He bids them throw away the present standards and look solely to the absolute will of God as it will be fulfilled in the Kingdom.

Jesus himself makes it clear that this is the nature of his ethic and is never tired of insisting that in the coming age all things will be different from what they are now. They will not only be different, but for the most part opposite. Men will have to reckon with an order in which the principles they have hitherto taken for granted will be reversed. Those who are first will be last. The kind of life which is here the wisest and most profitable will be mere waste and folly. It cannot be affirmed too strongly that what Jesus had in mind was not merely a steady progress by which the world will advance from its present phase to a higher level. All progress since he appeared has indeed been actuated by his teaching, but this does not mean that if we still continue to advance, in the direction to which he pointed, we shall finally attain to the Kingdom. The mariner steers towards the pole-star, but does not expect that if he only sails far enough he will at last reach it. Sailing round the earth he merely advances from one point on earth to another. Jesus bids us seek the Kingdom, and tells us that by seeking it we shall find guidance also in the present life. But the Kingdom itself will always remain unattainable.

We are not to think of Jesus, therefore, as an ethical teacher, whose primary interest is in the right conduct of life under the present conditions. He desires us to look beyond this world and live for the Kingdom. Again and again he says explicitly that the effort to obey him can have no other result than earthly failure. "If any man will come after me, let him take up his cross and follow me." The earthly order, with all its imperfections, is that which we must live in, and those who defy or renounce it are bound to suffer the penalty. This is fully recognized by Jesus. He impresses on his disciples that they must not complain if they meet with trouble, poverty, persecution, for they can expect nothing else. This world reserves its favours for those who accept its order, and this is only just. Nevertheless he calls on men to throw in their lot with the Kingdom of God, and live even now, in spite of all distress and calamity, as if it were come. Losing their life in this world they will find it. It must never be forgotten that when he made this demand he thought of the Kingdom as close at hand. Since the present order had almost run its course it might be left out of account. Men might cut loose from it and identify themselves boldly with the coming order, which was now the only one that mattered. He says in effect, "I demand of you what seems impossible, but the whole nature of things is presently to change, and this course of action, which appears so utterly unreasonable, will soon be the only wise and right one." He required that men should think in terms of the new age. They had grown so accustomed to this one that they could not conceive of anything different, but they must change their minds and become as little children. Even now, while they were subject to the earthly order, they must rise above it and look only to the will of God as it is done in the Kingdom.

It is this which gives greatness to the religion of Jesus. The demands of the higher world were for him so all-important that everything else was of no account. If men could attain to the Kingdom only by the sacrifice of all earthly things, then the sacrifice must be made. "If thine eye offend thee pluck it out and cast it from thee." Nothing must stand in the way of that utter obedience to God's will which is the supreme end of life. No other teacher has dared to make this absolute claim, and it cannot be questioned that in making it Jesus was right. If man is a spiritual being he must live in service to the higher order. Intent on the Kingdom, he will defy the world and the world will crush him; but at all costs he must choose for the Kingdom. Ideally Jesus was right, and his absolute demand will always lie at the heart of Christianity; and yet it will never be capable of a strict fulfilment. So long as he lives on this earth, man is bound up with the earthly order. Whether he will or not he is compelled to submit to its limitations, and they break him when he tries to escape from them. He cannot conduct his life in this world as if he were already in the Kingdom.

Here, then, we are to seek the true relation between Jesus

himself and the church which came into being after his death. In a real sense he was the Founder of the church. It arose directly out of his message of the Kingdom of God. The members of the primitive community were those whom he had called out of the present world to inherit the Kingdom which was now at hand. When they formed themselves into a church they were not conscious of creating something new but were only continuing the life on which they had entered while in Jesus' company. Now that he had died and risen again and was presently to return in his Messianic glory, they were assured, as they could not be in his lifetime, that the Kingdom which he had promised was close at hand. The church was thus the outcome of Jesus' message. It was the fellowship of those who had been called into the Kingdom, who were waiting for it, who were living as if the new order had now displaced the earthly one. This was the idea which called the church into existence, and which must always constitute its inner meaning. It is the community of the Kingdom, made up of those who are living for the higher order. The church as we *Sermon* know it may seem almost to have forgotten those visionary hopes which inspired its first members, but it still rests on that foundation. The Kingdom is at hand and men are to feel already that they are subject to its law. When this ceases to be its meaning the church will disappear.

At the same time there was another purpose in the formation of that early community. Jesus had proclaimed that the Kingdom was just at hand, but time went on and it delayed its coming. The old order which had seemed already to be a thing of the past was continuing, and was plainly destined to continue, no one could tell how long. What was the church to do in face of this unlooked-for difficulty? The law of Christ, to which it had bound itself, was that of the Kingdom, and under the conditions of this world could not be carried into effect. How was it possible, under the old order, to fulfil those demands which were intended for the new? This was the problem with which the church was confronted, almost from the outset; and in the effort to arrive at some solution it took on the character which it has henceforth borne. The church arose out of the message of Jesus, but it may also be said to have arisen out of the apparent failure of the message. Jesus had proclaimed the Kingdom and had created a brotherhood which should live for it and inherit it when it came. But it did not come, and the brotherhood which waited for it had to maintain itself in the present world. Unless it could be fitted somehow into the earthly scheme of things it could not hope to survive and fulfil its divine calling. In all times since the church has had these two aspects. It has stood for the higher order, proclaimed by Jesus, and yet it has fashioned itself as an earthly society, conformed to the order of this world.

CHAPTER III

THE INITIAL PERIOD

According to the book of Acts the church began on the day of Pentecost. On that day, seven weeks after the Passover at which Jesus had died, the little company of his followers was met together and suddenly heard the sound as of a rushing wind. A tongue of fire appeared to rest on the head of each one of them; they were filled with the Spirit and under the influence of this mysterious power went forth to proclaim their message. Luke has purposely invested the occasion with circumstances of awe and wonder, so as to enhance its significance. He wishes us to see in it a counterpart to the giving of the Law on Mount Sinai, when God made a covenant with His chosen people. But beneath the legendary colouring we can trace the memory of an actual event. At one of their meetings, some weeks after Jesus' departure, the disciples first became conscious of those strange powers which were henceforth attributed to the working of the Spirit. This day of Pentecost is selected by the historian as the day on which the church was born.

It must never be forgotten, however, that although a man's life is dated from his birth, it has had an earlier beginning. His birth, indeed, is not a beginning but a completion. That antenatal period through which he has lived unconsciously is by far the most important in his whole lifetime. It has determined for him all that he will henceforth be. He comes into the light a finished human creature, endowed with the faculties, the character, the personality which are to be unfolded during the years that follow. This was no less true of the church. Whatever may have happened on the day of Pentecost it only brought to a head the process which had been leading up to it. If we would discover how the church was made and what it was in its essential nature, we must examine with particular care that dim preliminary period when as yet it had no visible existence. The period was a short one, only a few weeks in duration, and yet it counted for almost everything in the after history of the church.

It may be said that practically nothing is known to us of those earliest days. This, however, is not true, for the memory of at least one tremendous fact has been preserved. It was in those first days that the disciples arrived at the conviction that the Lord had risen from the dead. The story of the Resurrection is beset with endless difficulties—critical, historical, philosophical—but one thing is certain, that the church was fully persuaded of the fact. We have to do, not with a myth created by fancy, or perhaps borrowed from an alien religion, but with a belief which was held by all Christians on grounds which seemed to them indubitable. It may be granted that new elements were drawn from various sources into the original tradition. Within the Gospels themselves we can trace a development from the relatively simple account in Mark to the circumstantial narratives of Matthew, Luke and John. But behind the tradition in all its forms there was the testimony of those who had themselves participated in the events of which they told. Not only so, but it was those primary witnesses who were most firmly convinced of the validity of their experiences. They

The Initial Period

stood out before the world as the men who could verify the fact of the Resurrection. They made it the central theme of their teaching. They proclaimed it with such evident sincerity that those who heard them were constrained to believe it on their word. Whatever we make of the story that has come down to us, it rested on some fact which for the earliest disciples was so certain that they accepted it as the very cornerstone of their faith.

It is to Paul that we owe the brief account which preserves the tradition in its most primitive and authentic form. He commences the argument of his great chapter on the future life (I Cor. 15) with a statement of how Christ himself had risen. The short passage (verses 4–8) is little more than a catalogue of the appearances of the risen Lord, first to Peter, then to other disciples, in groups or as individuals. Paul expressly says that he reports this list of the appearances as it had come to him, and again affirms, as he closes, that the account which he has given is endorsed by all the Apostles. There could be no nearer approach to firsthand evidence than this passage of Paul, written little more than twenty years after the event and recording the direct testimony of eyewitnesses, most of whom were still alive. The writer, moreover, is able to include himself as one who has shared the experience of which he speaks.

It is to be noted that Paul says nothing of the empty tomb and the incidents connected with it. Even if he knew this part of the tradition, which is questionable, he must have perceived that it was of quite secondary value, for the mere fact that a tomb was found empty could prove nothing. Many reasons why it was empty might be suggested, and none of them could be so improbable as that its occupant had risen from the dead. The only evidence that could carry conviction was that of some actual appearance of Jesus after his death, and Paul lays the whole emphasis on this. He tells how on six different occasions the Lord who had been laid in the grave was seen by his disciples. In view of these manifestations it was impossible to doubt that he was now living. It is highly significant that Paul puts the vision to himself on the same footing as the others. On the way to Damascus he had seen Jesus, not in the body he had worn on earth but in his radiant, heavenly body; and he leaves it to be implied that the visions of the earlier disciples were of a similar character. The whole chapter is written to prove that the new life will involve a new kind of bodily existence. What is sown a natural body will be raised a spiritual one. Those who believe in Christ will assume bodies of glory, and even if they survive till the Lord's coming they must all be changed, casting off their material bodies and receiving the heavenly ones which are the proper vesture of spiritual beings. Christ was thus transformed when he rose from the grave, and it will be the same with those many brethren of whom he was the first fruits.

It may be gathered, therefore, that in the original belief there was no thought of a mere reanimation. The disciples had visions of Jesus, the same in his personality as he had been on earth, but now a being of higher nature, clothed with a heavenly glory. Did those ethereal appearances correspond with something real? In all times since there have been some who would explain them from the heated fancy of the first believers, who cherished the memory of Jesus and persuaded themselves that he had come back to them in his habit as he lived. Modern psychologists have undertaken to trace out the whole experience. They point out that when an idea is intensely present in the mind it tends to visualize itself, as when Macbeth saw the dagger as a palpable object, with the handle towards his hand. So the disciples never doubted that they had seen Jesus, risen from the dead; but what they saw was a projection from their own minds, taking a visual form. The appearances which they believed to be real were only the outcome of their imagination. But the problem cannot be so easily disposed of. Psychology at the best can only explain the mechanism of that conviction which impressed itself on the disciples. Jesus, who had died, was again present to them; this was a fact of which they were certain. He had in some way "broken the bonds of death,"[1] and had made contact from the world beyond with his disciples living on earth. The method by which he had done so did not greatly matter. It might have been by some external manifestation; it might have been by some inward working of his spirit upon theirs, and the visual form may have been supplied by their own phantasy, as the interpretation in terms of sense of an inward perception.

Too much attention has been concentrated on the mere process whereby the appearances of the risen Lord may have been rendered possible. The real question is that of the fact. Did Jesus, by some means, subjective or objective, make himself known to his disciples after his death? They were convinced that he did so; and if this was true the method does not greatly matter. Peter himself probably could have given no coherent account of his state of mind when he received the first vision of Jesus risen from the dead. He could only have

[1]Acts 2:24.

said, as Paul says of his entrance into the third heaven, "whether in the body or out of the body I cannot tell."[2] The whole meaning of the vision for Peter was not in the mode but in the fact. He was conscious that after an interval of parting he had come again into personal relation with the Master whom he had known.

The real difficulty in the story of the Resurrection is not a critical or historical one, but the difficulty which always baffles us when we seek with our earth-bound intelligence to apprehend the nature of the spiritual world. We know that there is such a world, and that we ourselves are in some mysterious manner related to it. Yet it remains hidden from us, and we can never discover how it is linked up with the world we see. What are the conditions under which the soul continues to exist when it is parted from the body? How far can it communicate with those who are still on earth? By what signals can it suggest its presence across the barriers? These are questions which in all ages men have been seeking to answer, and which cannot be answered since they depend on a kind of knowledge which is withheld from us. The Resurrection of Christ is a mystery because it is bound up with that larger mystery of man's relation to the invisible world. All explanations of it are beside the mark so long as we are ignorant even of the first principles of those things which we are trying to explain. Nothing is certain except that the disciples were fully assured that they had seen Jesus in the days following his death. They may have described very imperfectly what they saw; they may not have understood the nature of their experience. But whatever it may have been it was sufficient to

[2]II Cor. 12:2.

convince them of the great fact that Jesus, whom they had known on earth, was still living in the higher world. On the strength of this conviction they built the church.

One thing is particularly noteworthy—that the appearances repeated themselves for only a limited time. Luke says explicitly at the beginning of Acts that "he was seen of them during forty days." In his Gospel he would seem to think of the visions as confined to one day, or at most two or three; but the longer period is undoubtedly in line with the original tradition. It is borne out by Paul's account in I Cor. 15, which allows for a series of incidents, spread out over a considerable time. One of them was the appearance to "above five hundred at once," and this large number could not have come together until the report that the Lord had risen had become generally known among his followers. Paul includes among the visions that which was granted to himself, perhaps a year later; but he admits that it was exceptional. The period within which the Lord had chosen to manifest himself had now come to an end. Why was it that the appearances were thus limited to a definite time, just at the beginning? The limitation cannot have been due to Jesus himself. If he had entered on his eternal life and was clothed with a divine power, he could not have been subject to any temporal constraint. There was no reason why he should not continue, in every time of doubt and difficulty, to appear to his people, and we might have expected that the whole of Christian history would be full of such manifestations as were vouchsafed to the first disciples. It is admitted, however, that even in that miraculous age the visions ceased after a few weeks' time. The favoured few who had received them did not, apparently, have the same experience again. It cannot have been that Christ was now unable to return to them, and the inability must have been in themselves. For a brief time they were sensitive to the Lord's presence, but their responsiveness gradually weakened and died out. Christ might return, and Paul was confident that he had done so to himself, on the way to Damascus, but the disciples were no longer capable of apprehending him.

This fading away of the visions might seem to bear out the theory that they were subjective, arising out of a mood of excitement which in natural course subsided. It is a familiar fact that in moments of high tension men have strange hallucinations; they hear voices and see apparitions, and act as they would never do in ordinary life. Another fact, however, must also be taken into account. What we are wont to call a mental disturbance is the necessary condition of all the highest experiences. In the normal placidity of life they do not come to us; there needs to be the moment of ecstasy in which we grasp in a moment the truth or the beauty which would otherwise be forever beyond our reach. The validity of the experience is not impaired because it is accompanied with that strange condition of mind; on the contrary, it is the very abnormality which makes the experience valid. It has come, as we say, through an inspiration—that is, by the only channel along which the higher knowledge must always reach us. Handel declared that when he wrote the Hallelujah Chorus he felt that he had been transported to heaven and was listening to the song of the angels. That, it might be said, was a delusion; his mind for the time being was disordered, and he ought to have been medically cared for until the fit was

over. It may be so; but the sublime Chorus is no delusion, and
without the mood of frenzy it could never have come into
being. So the visions of the disciples do not in any way lose
their value when they are put down to enthusiasts, moved with
a wild excitement and hardly responsible for what they
thought and saw. This is only another way of saying that they
were lifted out of themselves. If intimations were to come to
them from a higher world, they were in the state of mind
which could respond to them.

It cannot be doubted that this was indeed their mood in
the days which immediately followed the Lord's death. For a
moment they had been prostrated by the awful calamity, and
then came the reaction. They remembered that Jesus had
claimed to be the Messiah who was to bring in the Kingdom.
His death could be nothing but the means designed by God
whereby he would enter on his office. Instead of frustrating His
purpose it must in some way have accomplished it. The Kingdom which had hitherto been a distant hope must now be on
the very point of fulfilment. One of the distinctive features of
the Gospel of Mark is the prediction, repeatedly made by Jesus
in the days before the Passion, that he would suffer and die
at Jerusalem, only to rise again as the Messiah. It has been
argued that these passages were added to the story later, in
view of what had actually happened; but there is nothing improbable in the tradition that when Jesus warned his disciples
of his impending death he also taught them to look beyond it.
At the Last Supper he only repeated by means of symbols what
he is said to have predicted in words, giving his solemn pledge
to his followers that they would be reunited with him in the
Kingdom which was now at hand. When the terrible crisis was

over those who had listened to his promises could not but recall them. He had foretold his death, and it had come as he had said; they now awaited the victory which he had also foretold. In Luke's account of the two travellers to Emmaus we may discover a true analysis of the mood of Jesus' followers on the morrow of his death. They were dismayed by the blow which had fallen on them, and yet their faith was only waiting to be revived. When those two had at last recognized their unknown companion they said to one another, "Did not our hearts burn within us while he talked with us on the way?" They were already unconsciously aware of who he was, and in all the disciples during those momentous days there was the same thrill of expectancy. They were waiting for the Resurrection.

It thus belongs to the essence of the whole narrative that the visions came when the minds of those who received them were peculiarly sensitive. A mood of this kind could not be of long duration. Men are so constituted that they cannot escape for more than a brief interval from their ordinary selves, and even then the most trivial accident will at once throw them back again. According to the book of Acts the period of the appearances was about forty days, and the day of Pentecost may thus be taken as closing the initial phase of the church's history and inaugurating a second one, more impressive in its outward results but far less significant. It was in those first days that the church not only came into being but assumed the character which it was ever afterwards to bear. Historians are apt to take for granted that this brief initial time may be almost left out of account. It was only the empty leaf between two chapters of a volume. We may conceive of it, if we will, as occupied with the gradual recovery of Jesus' followers, as in a beneficent sleep, from the disaster which had left them helpless. This view may be justified in so far as the church of those first days had not yet wakened into consciousness. It was guided in its actions not by any clear purpose but by an instinct which it never tried to explain. Yet that short period at the outset was decisive for the whole future. The roots were forming out of which the church was henceforth to grow.

The visions of the risen Lord are not, therefore, to be taken by themselves. They need to be considered as evidence, not only for the Resurrection, but for that exalted mood out of which the church arose. During that short time at the beginning the disciples were in a frame of mind which they had not known before and were never to attain to afterwards. While they were in Jesus' company they had not grasped the full import of his message, and could only think of the Kingdom as remote and uncertain. In their later years it had again receded into the distance, as the present age reasserted itself and closed in around them. But for that brief interval after Jesus' death they stood as it were on a hilltop from which the end of the road lay clear before them. The great act had now been accomplished which would bring God's purposes to fulfilment. Jesus had died and risen again and entered into his glory and would presently return as Lord. The Kingdom was on its way; in everything except the final triumph it was actually come. In the age that followed, the disciples were to achieve great things, but they were never to regain the splendid confidence which inspired them at the very outset. As they ceased to have visions of the risen Lord, so they lost the faculty of apprehending the Kingdom as something that could be almost felt and seen. But for that little time they were completely lifted out of the world of sense. They had their being, as Christ's people, in that higher spiritual order which he had proclaimed. For once in human history the partition between the seen and the unseen was broken down. A group of men and women were seeking to live in the present world as if they were in that other world where God is King.

It has been the error of most church historians to think of the church as forming itself by a rational process. They have asked themselves at every point, "What was the purpose of this custom or institution? Why did the disciples act in this particular manner? How is this belief or doctrine to be logically explained?" Endless ingenuity has been expended in tracing back every action of the primitive church to its practical motive, and in searching the other religions of the time for analogies and possible influences. No doubt on the face of it this is the method by which history ought to be investigated. Man is a rational creature, and behind all his undertakings there is some design, which he seeks to carry out according to a reasoned plan. The customs of a savage tribe may seem to be utterly meaningless, but it can always be shown when we study them more closely that they are based on some kind of reason. Rome and London were founded in a dim antiquity, and we think of them as growing up at haphazard. Yet as we examine their natural situation we can still make out the purpose which must have been in the mind of their founders, and the processes by which means were adapted to ends. Columbus sailed out into unknown waters, but he made his venture on the ground of calculations, for the most part erroneous, as to the shape of the earth and the position of the continents. It is natural to assume that the church was formed in a similar manner. The early disciples created something new and strange, but they went about the work with an object more or less clearly defined, and thought out the methods whereby it might be attained. It seems obvious, therefore, that in order to explain the primitive church we have only to put ourselves into the place of the disciples, and consider what they wished to do, and the means at their disposal, and the models they were able to copy. All that seems obscure in the origin of the church will then become fully intelligible. But a method like this, though it may serve to elucidate most historical problems, cannot be applied to the primitive history of the church. We have here to do with something which was not the product of any design, and all effort to explain it rationally is labour wasted. The disciples in those first days were not deliberating and planning, but were seeing visions of the risen Lord. They were not providing by clever devices for the needs of the future, but were expecting the Kingdom of God to break in at any hour. Their minds were occupied wholly with the heavenly order which was now at hand, and all thought of worldly wisdom appeared to be mere folly. So in the study of the primitive church rational considerations are out of place. At a later time the work was carried forward by far-seeing leaders, who had definite aims before them and carefully thought out their measures; but they followed a course which had been determined for them in the days when everything was left to the free action of the Spirit. The church was like an island which has been thrown up by a convulsion of nature. A time comes when it is settled and cultivated and built upon; but when it first emerged it took on the configuration which it never loses, and which decides the character of all the later changes.

So we cannot understand the church unless we take account of the exalted mood of the first disciples. They waited daily for the return of Christ to bring in the Kingdom. For the time being they were lifted out of the present world, and felt that already they had part in the higher order. Old things had passed away; all things had become new. The church, it may be said, was the creation of an ecstasy. It did not arise from any set purpose to form a society for the promulgation of the new message, or for the replacing of the old Israel by a purely spiritual one. It arose out of a burning conviction that the Kingdom of God was all but come, and that men must break away from the present world and live for the Kingdom. This is the conviction which has lain ever since at the heart of the church, and which makes it different from all other societies. It is the community which stands in this earth for the higher spiritual order. Amidst all the changes which it has undergone in its government and doctrine and modes of worship and practical activities, this is its formative idea, and when it loses this it ceases to be the church. And when we look for the origin of this idea we can only find it in the rapturous mood which possessed the first disciples. They were sensitive in a unique degree to intimations from the higher world. They realized with a passionate faith that it was the one reality, and that they must forget all other things and set their hearts on it. The ecstasy soon passed away. It lasted in its full intensity only for those few weeks in which the visions of the risen Lord repeated themselves. Yet in that brief period the church received the impress which it has retained for nearly twenty centuries. A piece of iron is moulded when it is red-hot. Ever afterwards it remains a vessel, or a ploughshare, or a weapon, but it had to become so in the moment when it was liquid fire. So the church began without any conscious aim or plan as a little group of men who were caught up for an hour into a visionary world. Out of that mood of ecstasy the church as we still know it derived its being.

Comunnal idea in Christianity

It arose as a community, and there is a question here which has never been adequately answered. Why is the idea of fellowship inseparable from the practice of Christianity? It is no doubt true that for any important enterprise men must join together, and the church is sometimes regarded as simply an aggregate of people who have found it helpful to unite their effort in the pursuit of a common aim. As members of a great society they can make their influence felt and can set their hand to large undertakings which would otherwise lie beyond their power. They can also encourage and support one another, and become better Christians as they follow the Christian life in congenial company. Thus we are wont to think of the church in terms of the numbers that compose it. It is the collection of Christian people, and the larger it can be made the more it becomes a church. Individuals who are nothing by themselves are transformed into a mighty force according as they are fused together in this great mass of Christian effort. The church, however, is much more than the total sum of its members. Community is an essential element in the Christian life itself. Through his union with others every Christian obtains something for his own soul which he could never have had if he stood alone. The church does not merely receive from each of its members some addition of power and significance.

Sermon

It gives much more than it gets. It has a life of its own, quite apart from the individuals who happen to belong to it from time to time. As Paul recognized, it is the Body of Christ, and just as a hand or a foot is nothing when separated from the body so the Christian, cut off from the Christian fellowship, loses the vital principle which has made him what he is.

From the very outset the communal idea has been integral to Christianity. When Jesus entered on his ministry his first action was to attach to himself a band of disciples. Without this fellowship he could not have carried on his work, and his message would have lost half its meaning. The saying is ascribed to him, and certainly expresses his authentic thought, "Wherever two or three are gathered together in my name, there am I in the midst of them."[3] It does not matter how small the fellowship may be, but there must be fellowship of some kind, or the spirit of Christ cannot be present. This is an idea which underlies all the teaching of Jesus. He had come, not merely to win over a number of separate persons but to bring into a union those who believed in him. The name which he gave them was "the brethren," implying that there was a family bond which held them together. Most of his precepts are concerned, not so much with their individual duties as with their relations to one another. His final act was to hold a Supper with his disciples, consecrating them as a community which would cherish his memory and would be reunited with him in the Kingdom of God. After his death they continued this fellowship. In the few glimpses we have of them they are always together—in prayer, in study of the scriptures, at the common meal. As in Jesus' lifetime they are not merely a number of

[3]Matt. 18:20.

persons who believe in Jesus and look for his return, but "the brethren."

Why is it that the Christian religion from the outset has involved this idea of community? Many reasons have been suggested, all of them valid and weighty. Apart from the fact that men are by nature social, and must always stand in need of one another, it has to be remembered that in ancient times hardly any place was allowed to the individual. For all purposes of living men were assigned to definite groups and classes, and the man, severed from the group to which he belonged, had virtually no existence. This rule held good in religion as in everything else. Each religion was that of a tribe or city, and by their membership in this community the worshippers were related to their god. The idea of a Christian fellowship was no doubt affected to some extent by this ancient sense of solidarity. Again, it can easily be perceived how the teaching of Jesus led, of its own accord, to the formation of a brotherhood. He called on men to love and serve one another, and they could not do so except in a society. Christianity by its inherent nature has always drawn men into association. The monastic movement began, as the name implies, with "solitaries," who retired into the desert in order to live the Christian life without distraction. But they soon found that it was impossible under these conditions to follow the law of Christ, which called for the exercise of love, forgiveness, helpfulness. In the withdrawal from the world there still had to be community with others who had likewise withdrawn from it. Brotherhood, in some form, was of the essence of Christianity. Once more, it might be shown that faith itself, although it must be personal to every man, has the effect of bringing men into fellowship. "My own belief," said Novalis, "becomes twice as strong when I have found another man who shares it." This is profoundly true, and one of the great functions of the church has been always to provide this strengthening of Christian faith. "One Lord, one faith, one baptism, one God and Father of all."[4] The followers of Christ do not become fully conscious of their personal calling unless they can unite in repeating their confession.

None of these considerations, however, is by itself adequate to explain why the communal idea is so deeply rooted in our religion that the religion seems to dissolve when it is left out of account. Why can there be no Christianity without a Christian church? Perhaps the best answer to this question may be discovered in the light of Paul's conception of Christ as the "second Adam"—the progenitor of a new race of men. This was indeed the significance of the work of Jesus. Other teachers have aimed at some correction or enlargement of the ordinary ways of living. They have given their names to sects or parties, but their followers are distinguished only by their looking at some matters from a peculiar point of view. In all other respects they think and act in much the same manner as their neighbours. The aim of Jesus was to effect a complete transformation. Those who believed in him were to be different in their very nature from what they had previously been. They were to become as little children and enter on a new kind of life, based on a new principle. In other words, Jesus desired to mould humanity according to a different pattern. The "natural man," deriving his attributes from Adam, was to give place to this new type of man.

[4]Eph. 4:5, 6.

From this it followed that the Christian was not merely an individual who had put his faith in Christ. He was to be regarded, rather, as a single example of the new human type. He could not be rightly understood unless he was associated with the type to which he belonged. Now and then, in walking through the streets of a city, one comes on a person who is different in feature and complexion from the rest of the crowd. You know at once that although he is unlike the others he is no mere freak of nature. He is one of a race, and in some distant country there are multitudes like him. You cannot but think of him as lonely and miserable, away from those who speak his language and share his outlook on life. So the Christian is not only an individual but a member of a different race. If a day should ever come when there is only one Christian left in the world, men will indeed be puzzled by him. They will see at once that in all his character and behaviour he is unlike themselves. But they will recognize that although he is solitary he is one of a species. He stands for a race of men from which he has been severed. Somewhere, at some time, there must have been a human type of which this is an example.

Here then we are to seek the ultimate meaning of that instinct which led the Christians, from the very beginning, to form themselves into a community. In the last resort it was nothing but the affinity by which creatures of the same race are drawn to each other. Beneath the unity in hopes and beliefs and activities there was a deeper unity which may be described as one of kind. The Christians were reborn; their natures had undergone a change, so that they now belonged to a new type of humanity. It was only in fellowship with one another that they could rightly live their own individual lives.

The church, therefore, must not be regarded as something that developed later, and in some respects overlaid the message proclaimed by Jesus. His disciples, we are sometimes told, were not content with believing what he had taught. They joined together to form a community which assumed an ever greater importance in their religion, although it was only an after-thought and had little religious value. Christianity is one thing and the church is quite another, and the two must never be confused. The church may disappear, and some day will probably do so, but Christianity, as Jesus himself intended it, will endure. Such criticisms are due to a radical misconception both of Christianity and of the church. The purpose of Jesus was not to inculcate certain ideas about God and man's duty and destiny, so that we have only to cling to these if we would preserve all that is essential in his religion. He came to change man's nature at its centre, and so create an entirely new type of men. And the church is not a society of people who have agreed to accept the ideas of Jesus and maintain and propagate them. It represents that new type of humaniy which Jesus brought into being, and its rise and growth were inevitable, since it was involved in the primary intention of the Christian faith. The message and the community cannot be separated from each other.

So when we ask ourselves how the individual believers came to band themselves together in a church, we create a problem which does not exist. From the very start the community was implicit in the individual. A plant or bird or animal has no existence apart from its species. Its own identity is nothing but the species, manifesting itself in this particular form. A Christian, in like manner, is one with the new race of men which originated with Christ. He exemplifies in his individual life the higher type of humanity, and it is this which makes him a Christian. The church did not arise from the casual association of a number of Christians, for in a true sense the church was prior to its separate members. Jesus had created the new human type, and the Christians were those who were fashioned according to it. As Christians they belonged, by that very fact, to the church of Christ.

The church was thus involved in the Christian message, and there never was a time when the disciples did not think and act together. In his account of the first days at Jerusalem Luke lays emphasis above all on the sense of perfect fellowship. "They were all of one heart and one mind." "No one counted anything to be his own, but they had all things in common." Luke wrote in a time when the church had begun to suffer from division, and it may be that he has exaggerated the unity which had prevailed in an earlier and better day. But there can be little doubt that he has laid hold of a fact which had left an ineffaceable memory. In the days when the people of Christ had the clearest vision of the approaching Kingdom they were drawn most closely together. They were conscious, as they would never be again, that they were a new race of men, belonging to a higher world, and in consequence they felt themselves to be a brotherhood. There could be no surer evidence of how deeply the idea of community is implanted in the Christian religion. It did not grow out of any later reflection or practical necessity, but was given in the initial impulse. In a mood of ecstasy the disciples knew the Kingdom of God to be a reality, and in the same mood they knew that they must live for it as a church.

CHAPTER IV

WORSHIP IN THE EARLY CHURCH

The central thing in religion must always be the act of worship. It is indeed true, as all great teachers have insisted, that forms of devotion are nothing in themselves. There can be no genuine religion which does not express itself in the active service of God. But it is through worship that man becomes conscious of God, that he brings his own life into relation with the divine life. The power which urges him to acts of practical obedience is communicated by the approach to God in worship.

It has been the instinct of men in all ages to join together in their worship of God. Nothing, it might seem, can be more personal than the act in which a man withdraws from the world and presents himself, with his deepest needs and aspirations, before his Maker. This, however, may be the very reason why the sense of fellowship is necessary. In solitude a man is wrapped up in himself, and finds it hard to realize the larger, permanent issues of his life. Through association with others he is able to escape from all that is trivial and accidental. He becomes aware of the great human needs which lie at the roots of his nature, and which he therefore shares with his fellow men. "I pray," says the Apostle, "that I may comprehend with all the saints what is the length and breadth and height of the love of God."[1] The emphasis here is on the communion "with all the saints." By this alone can we rise out of our narrow,

[1] Eph. 3:18.

particular point of view and apprehend God and our own life in all the dimensions. We make our approach to God with that which is divinest in ourselves.

The Synagogue

The primitive disciples were accustomed to worship in the Synagogue. This institution was perhaps the most valuable gift which was made by Israel to the general life of the world. How it originated we have no means of knowing. It may have begun during the exile, as a substitute for the lost services of the Temple. It may have developed earlier out of the worship at those local "high places" which were suppressed when all ritual was centralized at Jerusalem. If it existed in any form during the ancient period nothing is said about it in the Old Testament, except incidentally in a late Psalm,[2] where the reference is doubtful. On almost every page the Old Testament has much to say about the Temple, which as we can now see was infinitely less important than the Synagogue. With its priesthood and sacrifices it was merely a survival from primitive times, and had its parallel in all ancient religions. The Synagogue was a new creation, growing directly out of the religious genius of Israel. Its purpose was to bring the worship of God into harmony with those higher conceptions which had arisen in the minds of the great prophets. God was invisible, and His worship was made independent of everything that was sensuous and external. He was the righteous God, and desired that men should serve Him by moral obedience. They were to meet before Him to meditate on His will, as it was revealed in His holy law. The rise of the Synagogue may be compared, in its historical significance, with the invention of printing, though

[2] Ps. 74:7.

in some ways it marked an even greater revolution. By the art of printing, knowledge was set free, so that all men could have access to what had formerly been the privilege of the few. The Synagogue made it possible for the mass of men to participate in the higher religion. Without it the work of the prophets would have gone for little. Their teaching, like that of the Greek philosophers, would have been intelligible only to small groups of the gifted and cultivated. Through the Synagogue a spiritual religion was brought within the reach of all. Judaism, Christianity, Islam, all religions which have based themselves on the higher conception of God, have modelled their worship on that of the Synagogue. It is bound to continue, under varying forms, as long as men interpret their religion in terms of the moral life.

The Synagogue worship was extremely simple, and consisted of three parts: reading of the Scriptures, in which God spoke to man; prayer and praise, in which man spoke to God; an address, in which man spoke to his fellow man. These must always remain the essential elements of spiritual worship, and the aim of a Christian service is still to allow due place to each of them. Jesus himself worshipped according to the forms of the Synagogue, and they were adopted, as a matter of course, by his disciples. From the outset, however, the church made certain additions to the Jewish forms, and it did so, not from any deliberate purpose, but in the unconscious effort to express the new Christian beliefs. It was through these new elements, grafted on the ordinary service, that the worship of the church assumed its distinctive character.

Before considering these modifications of the service it is

Worship in the Early Church

necessary to take account of one peculiar change which goes back to a very early time, and possibly to the beginning. Why was it that the sacred day was put forward from the seventh day of the week to the first? The Sabbath was the cardinal institution of Judaism, and the smallest infringement of the Sabbath law, as we know from the Gospels, was regarded with horror by every pious Jew. It might have been expected that the complete abolition of the Sabbath by the transference of its rights to another day would have been intolerable to those Jewish sentiments which the disciples shared with their countrymen. A change in the Sabbath meant an attack on the very citadel of the Law, and yet we look in vain in the New Testament for even the echo of any protest against this sacrilegious change. The controversy over circumcision almost rent the church asunder, while the transference of the Sabbath came about so quietly that nothing is told us of how and when it was effected. Among Jewish and Gentile Christians alike the custom was established, apparently without demur, of observing the common worship on the first day of the week.

We have here one of the most curious problems in Christian history, and many theories have been put forward for its solution. The customary explanation is that the new day was adopted in memory of the Lord's Resurrection, and there can be no doubt that the day associated with their primary belief was doubly sacred to all Christians. But the change cannot have been due to any mere sentiment. For Christians, as for Jews, the ten commandments were inviolable, and there could be no tampering with the explicit law of God "Remember the seventh day to keep it holy." There is, indeed, no sign that this law ever was set aside, and the change of day, it may be conjectured, has a simple and natural explanation. The primitive believers continued to observe the Jewish custom, and worshipped on the Sabbath in the Synagogue as they had always done. At sunset, however, the Jewish day ended, and there remained a few hours in which every one was still free from labour. Those hours after the close of the Sabbath could be used by the church for its own meeting. The day of rest was still continuing, and yet technically a new day had begun.[3] So after their Sabbath observances were over the brethren met for their common meal, and in conjunction with it held the Lord's Supper and their own Christian service. It followed the general lines of the Synagogue service, but allowed place to those new elements in which the Christian beliefs and emotions found direct expression.

To begin with, therefore, the Christian meeting was a sort of evening service, which rounded off the customary worship of the Sabbath. It was known as the meeting on the first day of the week, and when the mission spread to the Gentile world, and the Gentile reckoning of time was adopted, Sunday became the Christian holy day. This was the more natural as this day was already associated among the Gentiles with religious functions. It was dedicated to the Sun, the first and most glorious of the planets, and from remote times had been set apart for high solemnities. Jewish Christians, wherever they were, would continue to observe the Sabbath, but also met with their Gentile brethren on the first day of the week. Gradually, as the church became completely Gentile, the Sab-

[3]This solution to an old, and perhaps insoluble, problem has not, to my knowledge, been offered before, and may be taken for what it is worth. The best discussion of the general question is that by J. Cotton, *From Sabbath to Sunday.*

bath ceased to differ from other days. Christian reverence attached itself wholly to the Sunday.

It was probably in some way like this that the church was led to change its day of worship, and the character of the worship also underwent a change. For one thing, while the service was modelled on that of the Synagogue, each of its component parts was given a Christian colouring. The passage read from Scripture was no longer a section of the Law, but a prophecy which seemed to point forward to the Messiah and his work. It would appear, too, that from the outset the words of Jesus were placed on the same level as Scripture. The passage of prophecy would be conjoined with sayings of his which brought out its meaning, or with the recital of some incident in his life which had given it fulfilment. Prayer was offered, as in the Synagogue, but not in the stated liturgical form. It was uttered freely, on the impulse of the Spirit, and was presented in the name of Christ, the Intercessor. Christ himself was often directly addressed in prayer. Paul tells the Corinthians how he had "besought the Lord thrice" to relieve him of his bodily affliction, remembering, perhaps, how Jesus had healed the sick while he lived on earth. One of the names by which the Christians described themselves was "those who call upon the name of the Lord," that is, who invoke him in prayer. Hymns were sung, as in the Jewish service, but they were not the traditional Psalms, or later imitations of them. The Christian faith gave rise to hymns of a new character, often produced in the heat of the moment and almost as soon forgotten; but sometimes short lyrics of real beauty which were treasured and repeated. Such hymns are occasionally quoted in the New Testament, as in the verse, "Awake thou that sleepest and arise from the dead, and Christ will give thee light."[4] Paul expressly states that this is a quotation, and it is plainly Christian in origin and can only be part of a hymn. Similar hymns can be traced in the "faithful sayings" of the Pastoral Epistles and in the songs of the book of Revelation and of the opening chapters of Luke's Gospel.

As prayer was addressed to Christ, so he was often the object of hymns of adoration. This was so distinctive a feature of Christian worship that Pliny mentions it in his letter to Trajan as one of the peculiarities of the strange sect which he had encountered in Bithynia. "They meet together and sing a hymn to Christ as a god." This pagan evidence is borne out by some of the fragmentary hymns quoted in the New Testament. To this day, although prayer to Christ has been generally discontinued, he is still addressed personally in many of our most beautiful hymns. Most Christians would feel a hesitancy in offering prayer to him, and the same reluctance grew up, apparently, in the early church. The Fourth Evangelist declares in so many words that Jesus must not be prayed to, but that prayer must be offered to God in his name.[5] It is not easy to explain why prayer to Christ, which in ordinary form offends the Christian instinct, should become entirely natural, indeed necessary and inevitable, when it is expressed in song. From the first the believers used this outlet for their devotion. They held converse with Christ who was invisibly present in their meetings, and prayed to him in improvised hymns.

The worship of the church was thus modelled on that of the

[4]Eph. 5:14. [5]John 16:23.

Synagogue, while at the same time a Christian meaning was impressed on each part of the service. But there were other elements in the worship which were purely Christian in origin. Chief of all these was the observance of the Supper, of which we have already had occasion to speak. This, indeed, was not so much a part of the worship as the vessel which contained all the parts. The purpose of the Christian meeting was to hold the common meal, and to make it a memorial of Jesus' Last Supper with his disciples. That Supper had been his pledge that he would shortly return to establish the Kingdom. In repeating the ordinance the disciples reminded themselves of his promise, and it was this which determined the whole meaning of the acts of worship which followed. The worshippers were filled with a sense of the nearness and certainty of the Kingdom. They were able in some measure to anticipate it. In this meeting of the brotherhood they escaped from the world and were caught up for an hour into the coming age.

The worship was thus ecstatic in its character, and the distinctive feature of it was the exercise of the charismata, or spiritual gifts. Scripture had foretold that the advent of the new age would be marked by the outpouring of a divine power, the Spirit. This had hitherto been bestowed only at rare intervals on men appointed by God to some great task, kings, deliverers, prophets. A day was coming when the power from above would be the common possession of all God's people. "I will pour out my Spirit on all flesh. Your sons and your daughters will prophesy; your young men shall see visions, and your old men shall dream dreams."[6] The primitive disciples were conscious of a faith and ardour which lifted them above them-

[6] Joel 2:28.

selves, and awakened in them mysterious faculties of which they had not hitherto been aware. What could this be but the operation of the promised Spirit? A heavenly power was now manifest in the heirs of the Kingdom.

Of the new gifts the strangest and most impressive was the ability to "speak with tongues"—to express intense emotion in what seemed to be a real though unknown language. The phenomenon was one which has appeared not infrequently in the history of religion, down to our own day. When any emotion becomes so strong that it cannot be put into words, it finds relief in cries or sobs or ejaculations, and this is true also of religious emotion. But for some reason which has never been adequately explained the cries which afford an outlet to religious feeling will sometimes take on the character of an articulate language. It may be that the mind, groping helplessly for words in which to express itself, falls back on a mimicry of words, inventing them on the spur of the moment, and stringing them together in what appear to be sentences. However it may be explained the imitation of language is sometimes so close that even in modern times the *glossolalia* has been mistaken for a foreign tongue, which would be fully intelligible to some race in the past or in a distant part of the world. Luke appears to hold this view, and describes how on the day of Pentecost strangers from all lands were gathered in Jerusalem, and recognized their own languages as they listened to the Apostles.[7] Paul, however, is aware that the new form of speech has nothing to do with any that is used on earth.[8] To man it has no meaning, but is understood by the Spirit, through which it is given. He suggests that the "tongues" are nothing

[7] Acts 2:5–8. [8] I Cor. 14:2–4.

— 78 —

else than the language of the angels, so that the believer, under the impulse of the Spirit, prays in the very language which is used in heaven.[9] It was never questioned in the early times that the gift was supernatural, and its sudden appearance, so soon after the departure of Jesus, was regarded as a direct confirmation of the Christian hope. The disciples were waiting for the Kingdom, and now they had received the Spirit, which was to be imparted to God's people in the new age. It revealed itself in a manner that could not be mistaken by the gift of tongues, but this was only one of its activities. The believers could feel that in everything they had become new men. They were endowed with a fresh courage, a deeper religious insight, a new apprehension of God and of things unseen. All this had come to them through the Spirit, which Christ had sent upon his church out of the higher world to which he had now ascended. In place of himself he had given the Spirit.

The exercise of the spiritual gifts was thus the characteristic element in the primitive worship. Those gifts might vary in their nature and degree according to the capacity of each individual, but they were bestowed on all and room was allowed in the service for the participation of all who were present. "When you meet together," says Paul, "each of you hath a psalm, a teaching, a tongue, an interpretation."[10] Every member was expected to contribute something of his own to the common worship. In most cases the contribution would be a modest one, a sentence or two of personal confession or adoration, or perhaps a mere "Amen." But there were those who were peculiarly gifted with the Spirit and who prophesied or engaged in ecstatic prayer. It is difficult to make out whether

[9] I Cor. 13:1.   [10] I Cor. 14:20.

a special interval was allowed for those free devotions, or
whether they accompanied the service throughout. Paul is himself anxious that they should be confined within due limits.
He acknowledges the value of the enthusiasm, but insists that
although it breaks out spontaneously it should be held under
control, and he declares that this is possible. "The spirits of the
prophets are subject to the prophets."[11]

Christian worship had thus a root of its own. It was not
merely an outgrowth of Jewish worship but sprang out of the
new convictions which had taken possession of the church.
Jesus had proclaimed the Kingdom which was just at hand,
and the aim of his followers was to throw themselves forward
into this higher order. As they met together in worship they
could feel themselves set free from the earth-bound life. The
Lord had achieved his victory, and for those who believed in
him the Kingdom was now a reality. They were able to share
in the raptures and speak the very language of that heavenly
company in which their own brotherhood would presently be
merged. A worship of this kind could not long be maintained.
Nothing is more sincere than a high emotion, but it quickly
passes, and when the attempt is made to perpetuate it the result too often is some kind of make-believe. All that remains
of the original mood is the repetition of forms and words and
gestures which no longer have anything real behind them. This
was no doubt the reason why *glossolalia* and the other early
practices came to be abandoned. There are signs that they
lingered on till after the close of the first century.[12] They were
never formally suppressed, and again and again they have

[11]I Cor. 14:32.   [12]*E.g.,* various allusions in the Epistles of Ignatius.

been revived; and when the revival has come spontaneously they have had spiritual value as they had at the beginning. But it was felt increasingly that they were produced by a conscious imitation. A simulated enthusiasm is always offensive, and never so much so as in the sphere of religion.

Here, as Jesus himself was always impressing on his hearers, the one thing needed is an utter sincerity. God sees in secret, and knows the real mind of those who profess to be seeking Him. To approach Him with a pretense of fervid longing and devotion is the worst hypocrisy. A time came when the primitive type of worship had ceased to be sincere. Paul could perceive, before the first generation was over, that his converts at Corinth were using the spiritual gifts for parade and self-assertion. It may be inferred that even at that time religious emotion was deliberately cultivated, and before long the phenomena which had once seemed to come supernaturally were produced by a studied technique. This has been the fatal error in many subsequent revivals. They have begun with a genuine fervour, and have brought new life to the church by breaking with the formalism of ordinary worship. But they have ended by replacing it with a worse kind of formalism. Spiritual manifestations in which the Spirit has ceased to be present become a positive hindrance to the true service of God.

An answer may here be found to the charge which is brought so frequently against the historical church. It is alleged that after New Testament times the original faith died out and everything became frigid and external. An official ministry took the place of that of the Apostles and prophets; prayer was offered in liturgical form; laymen were excluded from an active part in the service; the accessories of religion were magnified at the expense of the thing itself. Not only so, but elements of pagan worship crept more and more into Christianity. The ordinances of Baptism and the Supper were assimilated to the rites of heathen cults. Sanctity was attached to symbols and relics and buildings. Art was brought to the aid of devotion, with the result that idolatry came back in all but name. All this, it is held, was indicative of a growing corruption which had changed the Christian religion into something which the first Apostles would have refused to acknowledge.

Now in such a view there is no doubt some measure of truth, but several considerations always must be borne in mind. For one thing, when once the church had undertaken to impress its message on the world, it needed to avail itself of every help which the world could afford it. By adopting symbols and practices which to the pagan mind were the necessary vehicles of religious ideas, it was not false to its own teaching. It was only seeking, in the one practicable way, to make its teaching intelligible. Again, it always has to be remembered that art is a language, just as much as a spoken or written one. To the Mediterranean peoples, with their inborn æsthetic feeling, it was the language which conveyed ideas most expressively. The believers who worshipped in the Catacombs were not conscious of any idolatry when the message of Christ was put before them in pictures. They apprehended it better. As they contemplated the picture of the Good Shepherd they were able to realize more vividly that Christ was still present and was guiding his people. Above all, the new forms of worship were indispensable when the first ardour had spent itself, and the spiritual gifts had lost their spontaneity. The aim of the church was now to cultivate the mood of reverence. Rapture, if it is to mean anything, must come of its own accord and only lasts for a moment, but reverence can be fostered and made habitual. Men can so dispose their minds that at any time they can turn to God and feel that He is near them. The church was intent, in the later time, on devising forms of worship which would produce reverence in place of the earlier enthusiasm. It surrounded its service with impressive ceremony; it threw its prayer into liturgies, couched in grave and noble language; as time went on, it devised beautiful buildings and stately music. All this was external, but the aim was to create the frame of mind in which men might offer a spiritual worship.

It is only right that we should recognize this motive which underlay the increasing emphasis on what might seem mere form and ceremony. As a matter of historical fact the development of ritual went hand in hand with the rise of Christian mysticism; and this was no matter of accident. It was the conscious purpose of the church to change the act of worship into a means of inner communion with God. The worshipper was made to feel, as he took part in the solemn observances, that he was in God's presence. He was called on to perform a number of outward acts, but in so doing he was conscious of an inward experience, and it was in this that his worship consisted. This conception was already familiar to thoughtful Jews of the Dispersion. It underlies the whole thinking of Philo, who seeks, with the aid of allegory, to interpret the Jewish ritual in terms of the inward life. Worship, as he understands it, is in essence a condition of soul, and the external acts have value only as they serve to reflect and to foster this condition.

From an early time Christian thinkers took up this idea,

which was felt to be in harmony with Jesus' own teaching. Paul speaks of a "reasonable service,"[13] that is, one which is offered by the mind. Men are to wait on God with pure thoughts, and hearts attuned to do His will, and only as they attain to this inward disposition do they truly worship Him. The writer to the Hebrews declares that all ritual acts are of the nature of types, pointing to a spiritual reality. Christ has now entered into a heavenly sanctuary and the old ceremonial has disclosed its true purpose. The people of Christ have passed with him through the veil, and have an immediate access to God. It is significant that the writer has nothing to say about any of the specific ordinances of worship. He indeed warns his readers against neglect of the customary meeting, with reference, most likely, to heretical sects which regarded all formal worship as now unnecessary.[14] But he prizes the visible service because it reminds the brethren, as they take part in it, that Christ has now opened for them "a new and living way." This mode of thought comes to its fullest expression in the great declaration of the Fourth Gospel: "God is Spirit, and they that worship Him must worship in Spirit and in truth." The whole of this Gospel may be regarded as an exposition of the idea which is here stated in explicit words. Worship consists in an inward fellowship with God through Christ. Forms and places, all mere external acts, are now subordinate. Christ is present in the heart of each believer, and in communion with him we share in the divine life.

It must never be forgotten, then, that this conception of spiritual worship underlies the apparent formalism of the later time. The early disciples were convinced that the Kingdom

[13]Rom. 12:1.   [14]Heb. 10:25.

was almost come, and this belief determined the nature of their worship. They were conscious of a release from the present life and all its restrictions. They leaped forward in a mood of rapture into the new age, when they would hold immediate fellowship with God. As time went on this mood no longer answered to a real conviction. There was no falling off in faith and devotion, but it was now apparent that the Kingdom was not to come immediately. What was needed was not the ecstatic mood but a settled habit of trust and obedience. It is important to note the change which now took place in the conception of the Spirit. At the outset the Spirit was associated wholly with the strange powers which manifested themselves in sudden visions and utterances. For Paul, however, these had become of secondary value. He thinks of the Spirit as an abiding possession by which the Christian is governed in all his thought and action. The whole of the Christian life is life in the Spirit. Exercise of the spiritual gifts had been the distinctive feature of Christian worship, and in a real sense it continued to be so. But ideas had now changed as to the nature of these gifts. One thinks again of that declaration in the Fourth Gospel: "The hour has come when they who worship the Father must worship in Spirit." For a member of the primitive church these words would have carried a well-defined meaning. They would have suggested that the time was past when worship was confined to a number of set acts and ordinances. Place must be given to the impulses of that new power which was now working in the church, the Spirit which expressed itself in tongues and prophecies. It is in a different way that the Fourth Evangelist understands the worship in the Spirit. He thinks of God as the invisible presence with whom the worshipper can hold communion in the quiet of his own heart. The one object in the later type of worship was to make possible this inward sense of God. Sudden raptures were now held in check, and all was done "decently and in order."[15] The worshipper was enabled without distraction to concentrate his mind on the eternal things. He was assisted in this effort by the accessories now grafted on the service—liturgical forms and symbols, an ordered ceremonial conducted by regular officers. These were only externals, but they served to compose and direct the mind and lift it into a higher atmosphere. There was a spiritual value in the very repetition at every service of the same pious formulæ and observances. Connected as they were with the act of worship and handed down reverently from one generation to another, they acquired a sacredness of which every worshipper was aware. Instead of reducing the service to a dead routine they provided a channel in which Christian feelings and aspirations could naturally flow.

It is thus wrong to assume that after the fervour of the early time, worship became merely formal and ceremonial. The spontaneity may have passed out of it, but in some respects it had grown more truly spiritual. The church had laid to heart Paul's new conception of the Spirit as manifesting itself not in spasmodic outbursts but in a constant mood of Christian faith and living. The primitive type of worship was bound up with the conviction that the world was all but finished and the new age was now breaking in. When this belief had lost its reality the church felt the need of a worship that could be sustained. It was indeed one of the great achievements of the church that when its early anticipations had failed it devised those solemn

[15]I Cor. 14:40.

forms, with the aid of which men could still separate themselves from the world and look forward to the Kingdom of God.

It cannot be denied, however, that the new mode of worship was fraught with a serious danger. Outward forms were employed as a means of awakening and supporting the mood of devotion; and this was wise and necessary. From the time of the prophets onward religious teachers have insisted that worship must be accompanied with the right frame of mind. If this is lacking the most impressive ritual can have no worth, while the publican who only beats his breast in heartfelt repentance will be heard by God. This is profoundly true; yet there has never been a religion which could dispense with forms of devotion. Just as thought must express itself in speech, so religion has need of some outward manifestation or it will wither and die. It is true in religion as in poetry that substance and form must go together. Nevertheless there is always a danger that the forms will take the place of the substance. It is almost a law of religious history that a faith originally vital is smothered at last by the ritual which was intended to preserve it. Noble liturgies have become a mere patter of unmeaning words; devout practices have decayed into superstitious habits; symbols once laden with spiritual import have grown empty. This has happened again and again in the history of Christianity, and almost every reformation has had for its object the discarding of an outworn ritual. The encrusting forms have to be broken before the spirit can be released.

In this work of reformation the watchword has always been, "Back to the primitive church." Worship in those first days was independent of all forms. The brethren simply met in some upper room and surrendered themselves to the higher power which moved within them. They needed no priesthood or traditional rules but offered the free worship of their hearts. But these efforts to revive the primitive practice have never succeeded. This may partly be explained on the general principle that it is never possible to restore what has once been. A custom or mode of thought may at one time have served its purpose admirably, but it was interwoven with the whole fabric of its age and all the old conditions would need to be re-established before it could be the same again. This principle holds good in religion, more perhaps than in anything else. In our relation to God there must be absolute sincerity, and we cannot rightly serve Him when we are living in one age and try to go back into another. Apart, however, from this larger difficulty all revivals of the primitive church are bound to fail, for the same reason that it failed itself. It sought to base worship on a mood of enthusiasm which could not, in the nature of things, endure. The fervid expectation of the Kingdom died away, and the type of worship which answered to it became forced and artificial. The church was saved because it learned in good time to adopt settled modes of worship. It ceased to demand that whenever they met together its members should work themselves into a rapture, and required only that they should wait on God reverently and thus open their hearts to His presence. It taught that this also was worship in the Spirit.

Yet it must never be forgotten that Christianity began as an ecstatic religion. While still in this world men felt themselves lifted into a higher one, and in this condition of mind they had glorious visions, and gave utterance to exultant cries. Religion has its roots in the conviction that beyond this visible sphere of things there is another, and the effort always has been to apprehend it. In hours of high experience or quiet meditation we can assure ourselves of its existence, and feel it pressing in upon our common life; but this is not enough. There is an unquenchable desire to grasp as a reality what we surmise or dream of. The traveller who catches from a hilltop a faint glimpse of the far-off city is filled with the longing to bridge the distance and pass within the gates. How can this desire be satisfied? From the earliest times one method has offered itself and has been practised in many forms. Religion has been associated with ecstasy, induced among the more primitive races by physical means, intoxication, whirling dances, dissonant music. Exciting himself into a frenzy the worshipper has been able to feel that he has broken through the earthly limits and soared into the higher life. Shortly before the Christian era this cruder form of ecstasy had been sublimated by the mysticism which had come in from the East, ultimately perhaps from India. A number of cults had found their way into the Western countries, differing at many points from one another but all turning on the idea of rapture as the one means of entrance into the invisible world. The theory has been widely maintained in recent years that Christianity was closely related to those contemporary cults, and it is more than likely that some Christian teachers, and especially Paul, were influenced by ideas and practices which they had made familiar.

It is certain, however, that Christianity had sprung from sources entirely different from those of the Oriental cults. In its central beliefs and motives it had nothing in common with them. Its character was permanently formed, even in matters of detail, before the alien influences can possibly have begun to operate. Yet early Christianity was akin to the cults in so far as it was, like them, an ecstatic religion. When the brethren met together they prophesied and spoke with tongues. Stephen beheld the heavens opened, and the Son of man standing at the right hand of God. Paul gloried in his visions and revelations. John in the isle of Patmos was in the Spirit on the Lord's day, and saw the things that would be hereafter. The condition of the early Christian worshipper was one of ecstasy, not compelled by artificial methods as in the other religions, but springing of its own accord out of a passionate conviction.

This mood may be illustrated from that which every one has known after the sudden hearing of good news. For the moment you lose consciousness of everything around you. You cannot control your own mind and body, and are hardly responsible for anything you do or say. Paul tells us that a stranger, watching the Christians at their worship, was apt to believe that they were mad;[16] and from Paul's own descriptions and those in the book of Acts a modern reader may get the same impression. Was there not something childish and absurd in those tumultuous meetings, where everybody was trying to speak at the same time, and no one could tell what the others were meaning, or what he meant himself? It seems strange to us, and not a little humiliating, that our religion should have arisen out of such beginnings. Yet we do not think it unnatural that at the siege of Lucknow, when the relieving army was at last heard in the distance, all who were left of the desperate garrison broke out into wild sobs and cries. In this there was nothing unworthy or ridiculous; how could they act otherwise in such a moment?

[16]I Cor. 14:23.

And the primitive worshippers acted in the same way, for the same reason. They had become suddenly aware of a great salvation, and were full of rapture, too intense to find utterance in words.

The ecstasy of early Christian worship was thus inherent in the nature of the message. Christ had won his victory and the Kingdom of God was now on its way. The believers knew themselves to be heirs of the Kingdom; they could feel that they were now standing at its very threshold, that already in some sense they had entered it. As they met together and realized the marvel which had befallen them, they could not but be seized with rapture, and the raptures could find no outlet but in inarticulate cries. The worshippers had ceased for the moment to be normal men and women, expressing themselves in rational language. Their condition was that of Paul when he was caught up into the third heaven, whether in the body or out of the body he could not tell.

The rapturous mood died out as the church abandoned its hope of the Lord's immediate coming, but it was never forgotten that Christian worship originally had been ecstatic. The feeling persisted that it should always be so, and from time to time the effort was made to restore it to its true character. Those revivals, for the most part, were allied with millennarian movements. It was believed that the hour of the Lord's return had only been deferred and was now imminent, and whenever this belief arose it produced a type of worship similar to that of the primitive church. Sometimes the note of rapture was recovered in a different way. For men of deep religious spirit, as for the Fourth Evangelist, the apocalyptic hope in its literal form had little meaning. The Kingdom as they conceived it was to be realized in the soul itself, and they sought to enter it by mystical contemplation. By this means they sought to obtain the beatific vision which would flood their whole being with rapture. At least for an instant they would be transported out of this world and share in the heavenly worship.

These efforts all broke down because they could result in nothing permanent. Worship is a fundamental human need, which cannot be satisfied when it is only possible at rare intervals, when the mind is stirred with a peculiar excitement. A service of reverence may seem cold and external, but it can be sustained and constantly repeated. It may not afford the exultant vision, but it offers a means whereby men may be conscious always, in their common life, of the presence of God. If the ordinary service appears to consist of little else than pious forms it may be answered that this is necessary. Without those forms there could be no stability and continuity in the Christian life. Yet it remains true that Christianity began as an ecstatic religion, and this must always be an essential element of its nature. The primitive belief in the nearness of the Kingdom was no illusion. It took an apocalyptic form, and was so far mistaken, but it corresponded with the fact, proclaimed by Jesus, that there is a higher order in which men are to find their true life. The church exists for the very purpose of witnessing to the nearness and reality of that other world, and if its worshippers could apprehend their faith in its full import they could not but know something of that rapture which possessed the first disciples.

This truth has never ceased to impress itself on the minds of devoted Christians. They have shared in the ordinary worship of the church, but have felt all the time that it was not satisfying. Tertullian was the most intellectual of the Fathers—the man who did more than any other to give strict definition to the Christian doctrines. Yet in his later days he threw in his lot with the wild millennarian sect of the Montanists. He perceived that with all their extravagance they had laid hold of a great truth which the church had forgotten. Christ had come to bring fire on earth. His message was one which kindled and inspired, and those who were content to serve him with a dull, conventional worship had missed his purpose. Edward Irving in modern times was an eloquent preacher who charmed a cultivated audience in London, but it broke in upon him that his methods were all wrong. If the Spirit had once been active in the church and had spoken in tongues and prophecies, why should it now be otherwise? The Spirit must still be present in Christ's people, and ought not to be kept down when it was burning to utter itself. Irving, like Tertullian before him, was disowned by the official church. He exposed himself to ridicule and made shipwreck of a noble life in his vain endeavour to bring back to Christianity that essential thing which, to his mind, it had lost.

It may be granted that these men and others like them were mistaken, in so far as they tried to recover the primitive ardour in just the forms which it had taken in the primitive church. To this extent they were unfaithful to their model, for the early disciples used modes of utterance which came to them spontaneously and which had no meaning when they were consciously imitated. Yet the main perception was a true one, that Christianity is, in its essence, an ecstatic religion. It began with a glorious hope which still burns at the heart of it, like the fires at the earth's centre. The world is passing and the Kingsdom is at hand; old things have passed away, behold all things have become new. This was the Christian message, and this it must always be, and those who have responded to it are lifted out of themselves. They are filled with a rapture which cannot wholly express itself in formal prayer and ritual.

The problem of Christian worship is to make room for this element of ecstasy without which it must always be incomplete. We have come to associate all that is irregular in worship with eccentric sects, or with illiterate people who are governed more by their emotions than by their minds. If their practices were introduced into an ordinary church service, as they were by Irving, intelligent men and women would be shocked and resentful. This in itself might be salutary, but there would be a danger not merely to the sense of decorum, which matters little, but to that of reverence. In the act of worship there must be no distraction. There needs to be order and calm around us if the mind is to withdraw into itself and concentrate on the eternal things. It is easier to draw near to God at a Quaker meeting than amidst the excitement of a so-called revival. Nevertheless it remains true that in the Christian religion there is something volcanic. Those who have caught the vision of a higher world are thrilled with emotions which demand an outlet. It is certain that in every Christian gathering, amidst the crowd of merely formal worshippers, there are some who are touched with rapture; their number is perhaps greater than we ever guess. How can a place be found in our worship for this ecstasy, which is not artificial but at least sometimes is the natural and heartfelt mood of the Christian man? If the mind of our time is growing dull to the meaning of Christianity the reason may be largely this, that in our worship there is so little of that fire, that active manifestation of the Spirit, which was present in the early church and which belongs to the intrinsic nature of our religion.

CHAPTER V

THE ORGANIZING OF THE CHURCH

The book of Acts is a work of history, but it is written, like the historical books of the Old Testament, with a religious purpose. It was planned by Luke as the sequel, or rather the continuation, of his Gospel. In that first part of his work he had recounted the earthly life of Jesus, who had appeared in an obscure province of a remote country and had travelled here and there with a small band of disciples, teaching and healing, until he finally went up to Jerusalem, where he was condemned as a malefactor and put to death. The book of Acts takes up the story where the Gospel had left off. Its theme is still the life of Jesus, but of Jesus risen and glorified. His company of disciples became a great multitude. It spread over Palestine, then into Syria and Asia Minor. Under the leadership of Christ and in the might of his Spirit it made its way into Europe, and found a centre in Rome itself. The movement which had begun so humbly in Galilee was plainly destined, in the fulness of the time, to conquer the world.

The purpose of the book, therefore, is to prove by historical fact that Christ was from God, and that his message was instinct with a divine power. In no other way could the marvellous progress of the new religion be explained. It has been customary, ever since Gibbon wrote his famous chapters,[1] to question this thesis of the book of Acts. Christianity, it is

[1] Chapters XV and XVI of the *Decline and Fall*.

granted, made an almost miraculous progress, but this is mainly to be accounted for by a happy conjunction of natural causes. Everything was in favour of the Christian mission. The world had been unified under the Roman Empire, and was looking for a religion in which men of all races could agree. Greek philosophy and Oriental mysticism were working together, and had created a frame of mind which was highly susceptible to a certain type of religious teaching. Jesus had appeared at just the critical moment, and though he was only the founder of a Jewish sect, which in ordinary course would soon have died out, his message had elements in it which were capable of a wide appeal. By a remarkable chance it was taken up by several men of extraordinary gifts, most notably by the Apostle Paul, who adapted it to the thinking and the social needs of the Gentile world. As a result it became the nucleus around which a universal religion was able eventually to form.

At this distance of time it is not difficult to advance such theories. After any movement has succeeded it always can be shown that the success was inevitable, and all manner of unsuspected forces can be discovered which were working to its advantage. But the truth is that Christianity, through the whole course of its early history, had everything against it. If it had failed instead of succeeding, there would have been no trouble in demonstrating that it was bound to fail. It originated among a people who were generally regarded with disfavour. Its Founder had been executed as a criminal, after trial before a Roman court. Almost from the first it was opposed by all the ruling powers as dangerous to the state. Not only so, but its teaching was hopelessly out of sympathy with the mind of the age. It defied those principles of reason which for all intelligent men of that time had an absolute authority. It stood for a morality which belittled the traditional virtues and threatened to undermine the whole existing order.

When we look at early Christianity with the eyes not of the modern historian but of the ordinary citizen of the first century, we cannot but wonder that it ever survived. All other religions were left free under the tolerant Roman administration; this one alone was persecuted, because it was plainly in conflict with all that men desired or believed. Why was it that in spite of hostility it went on from strength to strength? According to Luke it was because a divine power accompanied the Christian mission. Its Apostles had no help from without, and encountered every sort of difficulty, but the message they proclaimed was from God, and He endued them with His Spirit. This, for Luke, was the clear significance of the marvellous expansion of the church, and however we may choose to express it in modern language this interpretation of the early history is surely the right one. The triumph of Christianity cannot be explained from any combination of external causes. It was due to something inherent in the religion itself. A new power had entered the world through Christ and was working irresistibly through his church.

Luke is thus justified in regarding the outward progress as a visible evidence of the divine character of the message, but he is himself conscious that there was another side to the picture. He recognizes that with all the progress something was lost. In his opening chapters he describes in glowing colours the community of the first days. The disciples were filled with the Holy Spirit. Their faith was certain of itself. All were of one mind and heart, and no one counted anything to be his own. Everywhere in the book we are meant to perceive a contrast between the later church, with its hesitations and divisions, and the ardent brotherhood of the first days. This is no doubt due, in large measure, to the illusion of distance. Luke idealizes the age before him as the subsequent times idealized his own, which to himself appeared degenerate, infested with grievous wolves, not sparing the flock.[2] Yet his contrast between the early church and the later one answered to a fact of which all Christians were sensible. The church as they knew it was no longer what it had been in the opening days. It was prospering outwardly beyond the wildest hopes, but the glow and exaltation had passed out of Christian faith. Their religion for many had become a matter of routine, and almost of indifference. Ventures and sacrifices which had once been made gladly were never attempted.

There are many evidences in the New Testament of this decline which was everywhere apparent in the second and third generations. It may be partly accounted for by the reaction which always follows a tense excitement. Every high enterprise is launched on a wave of enthusiasm, and the most difficult things are done almost without effort. Then comes the ebb, and the work which was once a joy becomes painful, and can be carried forward only by a stern perseverance in some fixed rule. This was certainly the experience of the early church; but besides the natural lassitude it had to reckon with a sense of failure. The first disciples had been confident that the Lord was presently to return. He had died and risen again, and at any hour might appear in the clouds of heaven, bringing in the Kingdom. In this assurance the disciples had been

[2]Acts 20:29.

able to disregard the world they lived in. It had lasted its time and was now as good as over, and they would have part henceforth in that higher order which was to come. For a brief enchanted interval, following the death of Jesus, they lived as if they were already in the Kingdom. But time passed on, and the Lord did not return. The hope of his coming was never abandoned. It was believed that the glorious coming had only been deferred, and that there were those still living who would witness it. Late in his career Paul was confident that he himself would survive until Christ appeared, and that he would be caught up, in a body transformed, to meet him in the air. A generation afterwards the saying went abroad concerning one long-lived disciple that he would not die, but would tarry till the Lord came.[3]

But although the hope was never discarded, and has persisted to this day, it grew ever fainter. The church resigned itself to an indefinite waiting. For years, and perhaps for ages, the world would continue as it was, and there would be no manifestation of the Kingdom of God on earth. To many Christians in the New Testament times this meant nothing less than a shattering of their faith. The writer to the Hebrews laments the carelessness into which his readers had fallen in consequence of their disillusionment. This frame of mind was still more prevalent half a century later, when we hear of doubters who were saying "Where is the hope of his coming: for since the fathers fell asleep all things remain the same as they were from the beginning."[4] The church at large, however, maintained its faith in spite of all disappointment. It frankly accepted the fact that the Kingdom had not come as the first

[3]John 21:23. [4]II Peter 3:4.

1990

believers had anticipated. The world was not to disappear but was to endure as before, with all its hardships and restrictions. Christians had therefore to adjust themselves to these conditions under which they were compelled to live. Instead of trying to assume that the Kingdom was on the point of coming, they must learn to fit their Christianity into the framework of this present world.

The study of Christian origins has always suffered from the failure to define exactly what is meant by "the church." This term may denote the church in its intrinsic character of the holy community, the fellowship of those who have identified themselves with the Kingdom of God. In this sense it owes its existence directly to Jesus, and is bound up with the very idea of Christianity. But when we speak of the church we commonly have in mind the historical organization, with its creeds and rituals and schemes of government. The attempt is made to trace back this ecclesiastical system to Jesus himself. Since it is the church he must have foreseen and planned it, and the structure which arose afterwards was only the realization of his own design. Thus Newman put forward an ingenious theory of "development," using this term in much the same sense as that which it bears in photography. Jesus created the church, just as we know it in later history, but he left everything in miniature. The task of the artificers who came afterwards was to educe the larger picture which was latent in what seemed to be nothing but a blur. All was there, down to the minutest detail, but it took centuries to disclose fully what was hidden. This, however, is to confuse two different things. What Jesus originated was the brotherhood which waited for the Kingdom. This community of his followers survived his death, but it shortly began to assume a shape which he had not contemplated. The church was indeed the consequence of the work of Jesus, and at the core of it there is still the formative idea which it derived from him. But this idea and the visible organization are not to be confused together.

It would hardly be wrong to say that the church, in its historical form, had its origin, not so much in the message of Jesus as in the apparent failure of the message. Jesus had declared that the Kingdom was at hand, and his followers had understood him literally. They united in a fellowship which regarded the present world as in the act of passing, and which lived wholly for the approaching Kingdom. It became increasingly certain that this hope was premature. The Kingdom did not come, and if the fellowship were to continue it had to be placed on a different basis. Since the world was to last on, the believers must accept it. They must constitute themselves as a society similar in character to those around it and able to hold its own in the existing order. One thinks of the old explorers who set out confidently on the quest for El Dorado. They never doubted that it lay somewhere in front of them, just over the horizon, and on their march they built rude settlements which might serve as resting-places. The Golden City always remained distant, and as the hope of it faded those settlements took on a new importance. They grew in the course of time into the great cities which we know today. It was in much the same manner that the historical church arose and expanded. Like the explorers the early disciples set out with a magnificent hope. They formed the little community, meeting in an upper room, which would presently be reunited with

Christ in his·Kingdom. The Lord did not return, but the community endured and built itself up into the worldwide church.

At some time, then, while it was still confined to Jerusalem, the church underwent a momentous change. Luke, the earliest of church historians, is aware of this change, although he is still too near to perceive its full nature and significance. We can now see, much more plainly than he could do, what was happening in the time succeeding the day of Pentecost. The ·community of the Kingdom was transforming itself into an earthly society. Instead of holding separate from the world, the believers had resolved to accept it and to accommodate themselves to its requirements. This·change of attitude was not effected all at once. The belief that Christ was coming and that with his return a new order would set in was a fixed element in Christian faith, but more and more it fell into the background, or was understood in a purely spiritual sense. With this waning of the primitive hope there came a change in the character of the church. By degrees it took on the form of an ordinary association, modelling itself on others, both Jewish and Gentile, with which it was thrown into contact. At the beginning it had existed solely for the Kingdom, and had acknowledged no other control than that of the Spirit. Now it began to present two aspects, one of them directed to the Kingdom and the other to the world.

The outstanding mark of this change was the growth of an organization. In the initial period there had been no thought of an official ministry, set rules of procedure, a definite creed and method of worship. When the Kingdom came men were to serve God spontaneously because they were in complete harmony with His will, and the church belonged to the King-dom. It sought to make itself entirely different from earthly societies, which were held together by law and compulsion. "The kings of the Gentiles exercise authority over them, and those that rule them are called benefactors. But ye shall not be so; but he that is greatest among you let him be as the younger, and he that is chief as he that doth serve."[5] This injunction, attributed to Jesus, was put literally into practice. The church proclaimed its affinity with the new age by discarding all the trammels which are imposed by this one. Its members could feel that they were called into a perfect liberty, such as men would know when the Kingdom of God had come in.

For that brief period, when the brethren were few, and all of one heart and mind, and sustained by a high enthusiasm, the ideal was in some measure attainable; but very soon it had to be abandoned. The Kingdom had failed to come, and the growing church had meanwhile to maintain itself amidst the difficulties of the present age. Whether it would or not it had to submit to the restraints which all other societies had found necessary. It had to integrate itself with this world's order, which is based on law. Human society, like the whole frame of things of which it forms a part, must have law for its foundation. Even in a family, however the members may be bound together by mutual affection, there must be parental authority, set hours for meals, duties and possessions assigned to each individual; otherwise everything will go to pieces. The larger the community the more need there is for proper regulation, and in a great society, like a city or a state or an army, it becomes the one thing that matters. This was the truth which gradually

[5]Luke 22:25, 26.

forced itself on the church. It was looking for the new age in which all would be governed harmoniously by the will of God; it was seeking to anticipate this happy day, when system and authority would be things of the past. But it discovered, by hard experience, that so long as it remained in this world it must subject itself to law.

This became the more evident for the very reason that the Christian life, in all its activities, was brought within the sphere of religion. The church was not merely a company which met together for purposes of worship, but a brotherhood in the fullest sense. Its members were associated in everything they did; they ate together, and had the same interests, and were supported by a common fund into which each one had thrown his possessions. By means of this participation they sought to realize their ideal of the perfect society which would exist in the Kingdom of God. But the subjection of everything to the religious motive was perhaps the chief factor in secularizing the life of the church. The Spirit might counsel wisely in the conduct of public worship and the appointment of teachers and missionaries, but when material goods had to be fairly divided, when charity had to be bestowed on the right persons, there needed to be practical administration. Competent officials had to be chosen, books had to be kept as in ordinary business. If these methods were neglected injustice was sure to happen, and the feeling of brotherhood, which it was the aim of the church to foster, could not be preserved. It is in connection with the common fund that we first hear of dissension among the brethren, and of measures taken to introduce system into the affairs of the church. No one doubted as yet that everything must be done according to the will of the Spirit;

but it had grown apparent that the Spirit could not be left wholly to itself. There was a material side to the Christian life, and it required the methods which hold good for the material world.

Little is told us of how an official ministry gradually emerged from the fellowship in which all were equal, but it is easy to see how the way was prepared for it. In every group of equals there is some one who by his gifts or his force of character inevitably takes the lead. This was the position of Peter in the early days of the church, as it already had been during the lifetime of Jesus. Although he held no stated office he was accepted as the counsellor and spokesman of the church, and without him it could hardly have survived the difficult time when it was struggling for bare existence. Of all Jesus' disciples he seems to have been the only one of outstanding intellect, and with his ardent faith and genial temper he was peculiarly fitted to hold a band of enthusiasts together.

With Peter were associated the rest of the twelve disciples. As the personal followers of Jesus they had a claim to precedence which was never disputed, and were known pre-eminently as the Apostles. At an early date, most likely in the days immediately succeeding the death of Jesus, they adopted as their colleague James, the Lord's brother. He makes no appearance during the ministry of Jesus except on the one occasion when he joined with the family in an effort to withdraw his brother from an undertaking which seemed to them insane and dangerous. After the Crucifixion he threw in his lot with the disciples and was soon recognized as one of their leaders. At first this place would be accorded him because of his personal relation to Jesus, and "the Lord's brother" is added to his name as a sort of title of honour. But he gradually asserted himself in his own right. It is noteworthy that while the Twelve drop out of the history, as men are wont to do when their eminence is not due to their intrinsic qualities, James takes an ever more conspicuous place. He finally appears as the acknowledged leader of the church, to whom Peter himself is subordinate.

James has sometimes been called "the first bishop," and although the name is misleading in so far as it suggests a system which had not yet come into existence, it calls attention to a fact. More than any other man James was responsible for the organizing of the church. The place he occupied was not one of moral leadership, like that of Peter, but an official primacy. He appears as the president at church meetings, as the head of a body of "elders" who administer the church under his direction. He sends out delegates in his own name to enquire into the action of distant communities. For nearly a generation the mother church at Jerusalem was ruled by James, who impressed his individual mark on the church at large. From all that we can learn of him he was conservative and somewhat narrow-minded, though it must never be forgotten that with all his zeal for the Law he generously gave the hand of fellowship to Paul, who would otherwise have pursued his mission under serious difficulties. But whatever may have been his shortcomings James possessed in a high degree the organizing gift. Peter was the abler and broader man, and was certainly more in sympathy with the inner principles of Christianity; but for the new task which now confronted the church a man of different type was needed. The enthusiast and visionary gave place to the practically minded man.

It was the growing success of the mission which compelled the church to organize, on an ever wider scale. New converts were steadily pouring in, and without some efficient system the brotherhood would soon have broken up. As a result of this rapid expansion the civil and religious authorities had taken alarm, and the church was in manifest danger unless it could present a united front to all opposition. Above all, it was now starting on its great enterprise of carrying the gospel to the outside world. There are signs that even when the mission was confined to Palestine the field was mapped out, and teachers assigned to definite towns and districts. The leading Apostles, while resident in Jerusalem, visited the daughter churches from time to time, and kept in touch with them by messengers and letters. When Paul went forth to evangelize the Gentiles he followed a system, carefully adapted to his aims and circumstances; but he never suggests that he was the first to plan his work in this fashion. He indicates, rather, that he acted on well-established precedents, and defends himself more than once by appealing to the known practice of missionaries before him.

The growth of the church thus entailed an organization, and was felt to justify it. Paul makes it his grand ambition to have Christian communities planted everywhere, and with this end in view is ready to avail himself of all possible means. He is willing to become all things to all men. He is full of ingenious schemes whereby the new religion may commend itself to every race and class and make its position more secure. We cannot but admire the zeal of the great Apostle, and the states-

manlike method with which he pursued his aim. Yet there is
another consideration which must not be left out of sight. In
order to expand, the church had to abandon the ground on
which it had originally stood. It had claimed to be the community of the Kingdom, and had disowned all rules and pro-
grammes which might associate it with the present age. When
it set itself to conquer the world it had to make use of worldly
means. It ceased to look solely to the Kingdom, and sought
alliance with forces and conditions which belonged to the
worldly order. We have to allow, in justice to the elder
Apostles, that this was partly the reason why they viewed Paul
with suspicion. To be sure he was doing a great work. He had
carried the gospel to the Gentiles, and the church was multi-
plying under his hands in a manner that no one could have
dreamed of. But the older disciples may well have felt that a
success of this kind was dearly bought. A time had been when
the church had no ambitions in this world, which was nearly
ended, and looked only to the Kingdom of God. Paul, with his
scheme for a vast mission, had tacitly denied the hope which
gave meaning to the church. He was taking for granted that
the world was permanent, and was anxious to win its favour.
No doubt by his concessions and adaptations he had increased
the numbers and the importance of the church; but had he
not betrayed its principles? When we try in this manner to
understand the point of view of Paul's opponents we can see
that they were not actuated merely by a blind conservatism
or a rooted Jewish prejudice. They were concerned for what
seemed to them a vital interest of the Christian faith. They
were content, and this may surely be counted to their honour,
that the church should forego an outward success and remain

what it claimed to be, the community of the Kingdom, which asked nothing from the world.

This opposition to Paul, as we shall see later, failed to take account of his true attitude; but it has to be admitted that he was largely responsible for changing the attitude of the church. In his eagerness to advance his mission he was perhaps too ready to compromise. He broke away from the primitive idea that everything should be left to the free motion of the Spirit, and relied on discipline and order. If his communities prospered and were able to maintain themselves during his long absences, it was chiefly because he took pains to organize them. We can see from his Epistles how much of his activity was spent on matters of practical detail. He saw to it that every community should attend to its finances, that it should conduct its meetings in orderly fashion, that it should find appropriate tasks for each of its members. This side of Paul's work was preserved and developed when much of his spiritual teaching was forgotten, and the church took on more and more of the character of an ordinary society. It sought its models deliberately in the guilds and corporations of the day, and before a century had passed a Christian church was almost a replica in miniature of a Roman municipality. It had a body of officers graded like those of the city, clothed in similar vestments and bearing similar titles. The conception of a unique society, representing on earth the new order which would prevail in the Kingdom, seemed almost to have disappeared.

There was another side, however, to this process of conforming the church to the earthly conditions. While it was ordered and governed in much the same manner as any other society, it never gave up its claim to a supernatural calling. Its members were assured that by entering it they had allied themselves with a higher world and were invested with mysterious privileges. This is well illustrated by the Pastoral Epistles, which in their existing form are among the latest of New Testament writings. They come from a time when the organization of the church was far advanced, and seem to have been intended for the very purpose of defining the ordinances which were now considered binding. In the view of this author, writing in the name of Paul, and availing himself, most probably, of brief notes which had come from Paul's hand, the church is no longer a community apart from the world and subject only to the Spirit. It is a fellowship of people who believe in Christ but who also seek to do their duty as good citizens. They pray for the emperor and obey the laws and are interested in the general welfare. They are shrewd in business and have found that godliness is profitable for this world as well as for the hereafter. Yet the writer never doubts that as members of the church they have part in the heavenly order. Living on this earth they look for "that blessed hope and the glorious appearance of the great God and our Saviour Jesus Christ."[6]

It is a singular fact that the secularizing of the church went hand in hand with a growing insistence on its divine function. The more it adapted itself to this world the more it enforced its claim to a supernatural power and dignity. This, indeed, was the danger to which it finally succumbed. While changing itself into a worldly institution it yet magnified its title to be above the world. It required that all those things which belonged to its outward organization—ceremonies, offices, build-

[6]Titus 2:13.

ings, robes and insignia—should be accounted holy. They had been borrowed from the world, to adapt the church to earthly conditions, and now they were revered for their own sake, as part of the higher order. In this manner the primitive conception of the church as representing on earth the Kingdom of God was almost reversed. A mere earthly power was invested with a divine sanction.

It is not surprising, therefore, that later reformers in almost every age have fixed on the organization of the church as the prime cause of all its errors. They have set themselves to break up the whole ecclesiastical system and so recover the original idea of a free brotherhood controlled by the Spirit. In so far as their efforts have been successful they have only resulted in the overthrow of some existing system to put another in its place. However we may strive to restore it, the free community of the primitive days is gone beyond recall. It was only the other side of the belief that this world is on the point of closing and is to be followed almost immediately by the inauguration of the Kingdom. A belief of this kind is now impossible, and had already become so before the first generation was past. The world is here to stay, and we have no choice but to reconcile ourselves to the plain fact. If there is to be a church at all it must somehow be conformed to the present order. Planted in this world it must submit to the world's conditions.

It cannot be denied that when it allowed itself to be organized the church was in many ways a loser. Not only did it surrender much of its freedom but it abandoned what seemed to be vital elements of its faith. It confessed that the Kingdom which it hoped for was still far distant. It acknowledged also that the demands of Jesus were as yet impracticable. He had called for obedience to God's will as it would be done in the Kingdom, but this could be attempted only if the Kingdom were now in sight. If men were still to be subject to the old order they could at best obey the precepts of Jesus in some qualified manner, with due regard to what was possible within the earthly limitations. Here again we have striking evidence of the new Christian attitude in the Pastoral Epistles. The writer addresses himself to a church now fully organized, and seeks to impress on it the ethical principles by which Christians must order their lives. His ethic is indeed a lofty and exacting one, and if all Christians tried to live up to it the church would have good reason to feel satisfied. Yet every one who examines it has the uneasy sense that it is a compromise. This teacher does not say, as Jesus had done, "Forgive without reserve; be absolutely unselfish and sincere and merciful." His demand is rather, "Practise goodness as much as you can; remember that you have part in a higher order, but do not forget that you are tied to this world and must take account of its necessities." As we trace the history of the organized church we can see that at all times it has followed this rule of compromise. Instead of taking its stand on ideal principles it has allowed for circumstances, for opposing forces, for peril that might befall the general welfare if any principle should be pushed too far. The weakness of the church has always been that while it stands for the Kingdom it is also an earthly society, which must keep step with the world at its side. However pure its motives, it cannot but lay itself open to the reproach of inconsistency, lukewarmness, hypocrisy.

Against the loss, however, we must set the gain, which has

been no less indubitable. For one thing, if it had failed to organize itself the church could not have survived. It began with a mighty ardour of faith whereby it was carried triumphantly through the initial dangers which might so easily have crushed it. But all enthusiasms are short-lived, and if it had trusted wholly to that early mood it would soon have dissolved, like so many ecstatic sects in the years since. In good time the brotherhood was changed into a regular society. It was now independent of sudden emotions, which might come and go. It had lost the early inspiration, but each of its members had his task appointed him, and as all worked together, under wise direction, the cause was maintained and went steadily forward. Not only so, but by organizing its life and worship the church made permanent channels for all Christian activity. Sometimes they ran dry, and there was little but the hollow routine of form and custom. But whenever the Spirit revived it found the channel prepared for it, and the life-giving stream was not dissipated and lost.

Again, as an organized society the church was able to throw itself into the active life of the world. If it had held to its first intention and looked solely to the Kingdom which was at hand, it would either have died out or survived as a hermit community. Like the Essenes, to whom they have sometimes been compared, the Christian brethren might have retired to the wilderness, with their message unknown to all outside of their own circle. Instead of that, when they realized that the world would continue they joined hands with the world. They mingled freely with their fellow men. They met the age on its own ground, and took their place as a society, framed on a familiar pattern and working by methods which every one could understand. The church thus made itself an integral part of the world's life, and to this it owed its wonderful expansion. While remaining the holy community it was not aloof and exotic. It shared in the common interests, and built itself into the social structure of the time. In this manner it took hold of the world from within, and was able to permeate and transform it.

Once more, by its change of attitude the church was better qualified, in not a few respects, to carry out the work of Jesus. He had indeed proclaimed a Kingdom which was not of this world, but in his own ministry he had not secluded himself in the desert, like John the Baptist. He had consorted with men in their cities and marketplaces, and had made himself the friend of publicans and sinners. The church could feel that in allying itself with the ordinary life it was faithful to his example. He had become one with men that he might enlighten and save them, and his church must do likewise. From an early time the idea grew up that the church was the new incarnation of Christ. As the divine nature had assumed the form of man, so the holy community, in which Christ reigned, was in outward appearance a society like others. Paul, as we shall see, makes much of this conception of the Body of Christ, and it is significant that he connects it, in the closest manner, with his demand for church organization. The body is made up of many members, each with its peculiar function, and all are so interrelated that they work harmoniously together towards a common purpose. So in the church there are diversities of gifts, and each member of it must be assigned his place according to his special gift. When it is thus knit together as a perfect organism the church becomes truly the Body of Christ, and will represent him in the world and bring his work to fulfilment.

Finally, it is not too much to say that by adapting itself to the earthly conditions the church grew to a fuller knowledge of that Kingdom of God to which it aspired. To apprehend any ideal there must always be some endeavour to realize it in concrete form. No one can understand great painting unless he has himself tried to make a picture. It may be only a wretched daub, but he learns from its very shortcomings what a true picture ought to be. The best reward of attempting any piece of work is the clearer perception of how it should be done, and the power of admiring those who have done it perfectly. Most of all in the moral life there can be no real feeling for goodness without the endeavour to practise it in everyday conduct. The selfish, indolent man may sentimentalize about the saint or hero, but can never even dimly understand him. It is the effort on your own part to act as he did, on however small a scale, which opens your eyes to the vision which he followed. We have here a principle which is too often forgotten in those criticisms of the church with which every one is familiar. It claims to represent the Kingdom of God, but how miserably it has failed. Its history has been little more than a long succession of bigotries and compromises, of infidelities to the high standards which it has professed to honour. Between the aims of the church and the actual performance there has always been a tragic contrast.

All these criticisms are true, but the answer is that by its failures the church has advanced to a better comprehension of what it seeks to be. If it had remained as it was at first, a company of enthusiasts who waited in a rapture for the Kingdom, it would have waited in vain, and would have forgotten in a short time what it was looking for. But when the Kingdom did not come the disciples set themselves to establish the church. They accepted the world as it was, and formed a community which would be part of it, and which would yet strive, under the earthly conditions, to live for the higher order. Luke tells us, in the prelude to his history,[7] how a voice came to the waiting disciples, "Ye men of Galilee, why stand ye gazing up into heaven?" They had begun with the confident hope that a new age was on the point of dawning; then they were disillusioned, and turned to the present world. They seemed to lose sight of the Kingdom as they sought patiently to build up the earthly church, but through this labour on the task before them they learned the meaning of the vision.

[7]Acts 1:11.

CHAPTER VI

TEACHING IN THE EARLY CHURCH

In the thought of Jesus there is almost nothing that properly can be called theological. By picture and parable he sought to reveal the nature of the higher world. He had himself apprehended it by immediate vision, and his aim was to make it real, in the same manner, to others. It is very remarkable that he hardly touches on the problems which have occupied theologians in all ages. He offers no proof of the existence of God, for no doubt of it seems ever to have crossed his mind. He never says whether he conceived of God as transcendent or immanent, as mind or being or energy. He believes in immortality, but makes no attempt to find a ground for it in the nature of the soul. Most of his teaching is concerned with the moral law, but he is content to take it for granted and has nothing to say about its ultimate sanctions.

The whole message of Jesus centred on the Kingdom of God, and it is commonly assumed that he had thought out this conception and formed a consistent theory. The questions are therefore raised "Did he conceive of the Kingdom as present or future? Did he fully accept the apocalyptic view? When and how did he expect the Kingdom to come?" Such questions, however, are beside the mark, for he seems never to have systematized his idea. He simply realized the fact of a higher order which men must live for, and which will finally prevail. It is, indeed, misleading to speak of Jesus as a "teacher."

The term goes back to the Gospels, but there carries the suggestion that he was the bearer of a divine message. It is never meant to signify that his purpose was merely to instruct, imparting to others the fruits of his own reflection. In modern religious literature a great deal is made of the fact that Jesus was a "teacher," and did not claim to be anything else. From this it is inferred that his true place is with the philosophical thinkers, from whom we have much to learn but whose ideas may be rejected when they are insufficiently proved or in conflict with later knowledge. But Jesus never professed to have arrived at certain new ideas which he wished to demonstrate to his hearers. His aim was to impress on men the reality of God and of the unseen world. Mark tells us that he called his disciples "that they might be with him"[1]—not to take in the information which he had to offer but by knowing him to acquire his attitude of mind. He was certain of the Kingdom of God, and sought to inspire his followers with the same confidence.

This assurance of the Kingdom was what Jesus had given to the disciples, and in the power of their faith they formed the brotherhood of those who waited for the Kingdom. New members were continually drawn into it, and were adopted by a rite of baptism. Jesus himself had not practised this rite, but it was employed, apparently from the outset, by his followers. All of them, perhaps, had undergone the baptism of John, as Jesus himself had done, and they assumed as a matter of course that it was necessary for those who aspired to enter the Kingdom. One change, however, was now introduced into the rite. Since Jesus was the Messiah of the Kingdom the convert

[1]Mark 3:14.

was baptized in his name, and was required to utter the confession "Jesus is Lord."[2] In so far as the primitive church had any creed it was limited to this confession, which was not so much a statement of belief as a declaration of loyalty. The Kingdom was to come through Jesus, and he would receive into it those whom he acknowledged as his people. The convert gave his solemn pledge that he was one of them. Nothing but this was necessary for admission into the church. The bond by which its members were held together was not an intellectual or doctrinal one, but a common assurance that Jesus was the Messiah who would presently bring in the Kingdom.

It was evident, however, from the first, that this faith necessitated some kind of teaching. The disciples themselves had acquired the faith unconsciously. In their intercourse with Jesus it had been impressed on them, beyond the possibility of doubt, that his words and actions had carried with them a divine authority. When he had asked them at Cæsarea Philippi "Who say ye that I am?" Peter had at once answered, in the name of all, "Thou art the Messiah." He had never told them so; he had proclaimed the Kingdom, but of himself and his relation to it he had said nothing. Yet the conviction had grown up in them, knowing him as they did, that he could be no other than the promised Messiah. How were they to communicate this faith to those who had never known him, or had seen him only casually? Mere assertion was useless, for at once the question arose, "how can we believe that this is true?" The men whom Jesus had called "that they might be with him" had in some way to prove to others what for themselves required no proof.

[2]Paul's use of this formula clearly indicates that it was the baptismal confession. *Cf.* Rom. 10:9; I Cor. 12:3; Phil. 2:11.

Teaching in the Early Church

Among the records which have come down to us of life in the primitive church, perhaps the most valuable is contained in a single verse of the opening section of Acts: "And they continued stedfastly in the Apostles' teaching, and in fellowship, and in breaking of bread and in prayers."[3] These are singled out as the chief activities of the new community. Its members lived in the closest fellowship with each other; they observed the Supper; they held meetings for prayer, presumably of an ecstatic nature; and along with all of this they received some regular instruction from the immediate disciples. What was the character of this instruction? There was only one subject which the Apostles could be expected to teach. As the personal followers of Jesus they alone could witness, with full authority, to his acts and words. When Peter was ordered by the Council to cease disturbing the people, his answer was: "We cannot but speak the things which we have seen and heard."[4] Here, it can hardly be doubted, we are to seek the fountainhead of the record preserved to us in the Gospels. Luke tells us in his prologue that he derives his knowledge from Christian teachers before him, who in their turn had listened to the eyewitnesses. His object, he says, is to sum up in orderly fashion the instruction which his friend Theophilus had already received. All converts at that later day were required to learn the chief facts of the life of Jesus and his cardinal sayings, and this, we may infer, had been the rule of the church from the beginning. In the earliest time the disciples themselves naturally had been the teachers. They could speak at first hand of the ministry of Jesus and of the impression he had made on those who stood nearest to him. This

[3]Acts 2:42. [4]Acts 4:20.

presentation of him as he actually had been was the most convincing proof that his claims were true.

There was another proof, however, on which an almost equal emphasis was laid. For the Jewish mind the final test of every belief was the word of Scripture. It has been well said that for the Jews in the time of Christ the Scriptures had much the same place which we now assign to mathematical law. A scientific theory is proved for us when it can be placed on a mathematical basis, and in the same manner a devout Jew was satisfied when the thing he was asked to believe was in correspondence with Scripture. Beyond the word of God Himself there could be no appeal. It was therefore imperative for the early teachers to adduce a scriptural proof for all that they affirmed concerning Jesus. In the Gospel of Matthew almost every incident is accompanied with the formula, "that the Scripture might be fulfilled," and this is no doubt an inheritance from primitive custom. Along with their instruction in the facts of the life of Jesus the disciples tried to demonstrate that in everything he did he gave fulfilment to Old Testament prediction. God, by His own infallible word, had marked him out as the Messiah.

It is important to note that from the very outset one of the chief activities of the church was this one of instruction. The first believers have often been represented as nothing more than a group of enthusiasts, carried away by strange beliefs which they had no means or desire of testing. Later on there appeared teachers like Paul, who sought to discover some kind of basis for the faith, but the original Apostles accepted everything without enquiry. Are we not expressly told that the Jewish Council "perceived them to be unlearned and ignorant men"?[5] This, however, was the judgment of a professional class, accustomed to think slightingly of all outsiders who dared to form opinions without the proper academical training. The same judgment has been pronounced later, by men of the same type, on Shakespeare, Bunyan, Burns, and many others of the greatest minds. The Apostles may never have studied in the Rabbinical schools, but they were men of more than usual intelligence; this must have been one of the reasons why Jesus selected them out of a large number who offered to be his disciples. As the church grew under their supervision they took on them the work of teaching. Not only did they record the facts about Jesus, but they tried to explain these facts in the light of the divine plan. From the very start the church made an appeal to the intelligence. It seemed to be made up of fanatical people, who held tumultuous meetings at which they fell into ecstasies and spoke with tongues; and we cannot but wonder sometimes that this movement began shortly afterwards to produce a succession of great thinkers who linked their beliefs to the loftiest speculations. But this was fully in line with the original tradition. Those primitive enthusiasts were at the same time teachers, intent on finding reasons for their faith. Peter, on the day of Pentecost, was furnished with arguments. Stephen went out among the Synagogues, answering all disputants and more than holding his own. There never was a time when the exercise of the mind was not one of the primary interests of the church.

The earliest teaching, as we know from examples of it in the book of Acts, was all based, in the Jewish manner, on the evidence of Scripture. This does not mean that as yet there was

[5]Acts 4:13.

no effort to think out the message, and that believers were willing to accept it on the bare authority of an Old Testament text. We are familiar in modern times with the Christian "who knows, and knows alone, his Bible true," and while we admire his simple faith and sincerity, we do not take him seriously as a religious thinker. But it needs to be remembered that all thinking among the Jews was scriptural. The Old Testament provided the necessary data with which the intelligence worked, and out of which it constructed the most far-reaching theories. In later times the Jewish mind has done marvellous things in philosophy, science, legal and political enquiry, but perhaps its highest achievement is still to be found in the great literature which enshrines its interpretation of Scripture. Much of the thought is to our minds arbitrary, or hardly intelligible, but there can be no denying its sheer intellectual power. If thought, like art, has a value for its own sake, quite apart from the matter it deals with, some of those Jewish expositors must be classed among the most gifted of all thinkers. In the New Testament itself, most notably in the Epistle to the Hebrews and some sections of Paul's letters, we have splendid examples of religious thinking, accomplished by a purely scriptural method. The earliest teachers confined themselves to this method but addressed themselves just as truly to the intelligence in their presentation of Christian truth.

This is a fact which needs to be emphasized, for in the modern study of Christian origins a sharp distinction is usually drawn between the primitive teaching and that of the age that followed. It is assumed by many writers that the later Christianity had little in common with the earlier except the name. The mind of the primitive church, as they conceive it, was childish and unreflecting. Paul and his successors took hold of the crude, traditional beliefs and thought them out in their deeper implications; and in this process the religion entirely changed its character. Such a view, it may be frankly said, is based on a misunderstanding. The church had always been conscious of deeper meanings in its beliefs. Teachers like Stephen had sought to elucidate them, and had brought to the task an intellectual energy hardly inferior to that of Paul. Again and again, for that part, Paul himself insists that he was no innovator. He declares that he taught the same message as the other Apostles and tried like them to interpret it in the light of the divine purpose. The only difference was that while the older teachers had used the scriptural method Paul had combined it with others, borrowed from Gentile thought. As a Jew of the Dispersion he followed the practice of foreign-born Jews to whom the Gentile modes of reasoning had become as natural as those of the Rabbinical schools. His right to do this was never questioned. The teachers at Jerusalem had misgivings as to his free attitude to the Law, but gave him the right hand of fellowship. They acknowledged that while at some points he differed from them he was a teacher like themselves, continuing in his own manner their task of expounding the gospel.

It is wrong, therefore, to say that Christianity in the later time was theological, while in the earlier days it was not. The only distinction was that theology ceased to be purely scriptural. For Jewish thinkers the word of Scripture was final. God had made His own pronouncement, and what He had said must be accepted as the truth. For Greek thinkers the ultimate

criterion was reason. It was the grand achievement of the
Greeks that they were the first to perceive that the world is
rational, that the mind of man corresponds in some way to the
universal mind. Nothing, therefore, could be accepted as true
unless it could be reconciled with principles inherent in human
reason. This rule was applied by the Greeks in every domain
of thought and action, and in the strength of it they built up
a new world of knowledge. They demanded that religion itself
should conform to rational principles, and in Stoicism, which
was the reigning philosophy of the first century, God was
identified with reason. There were many religions, worship-
ping God under different names, but in all of them He was
ultimately the mind which pervades the universe and becomes
conscious of itself in man. The one task of man, for the Stoics,
was to bring the reason which was in himself into harmony
with the divine reason. Philo of Alexandria, with his Jewish
religious instinct, could not accept this deification of reason.
Allowing that it was of divine nature he made it subordinate
to God—an outflowing of the absolute Being who Himself
transcends the world, which through His reason He has made.
Philo is typical of a mode of thought which was gaining
ground everywhere in the first century. Just as we are realiz-
ing now that there are limitations to science, so in the Greek
world there was a reaction against philosophy. Men had grown
aware that with all its effort it had failed to answer the fundamental questions, and that no answer to them was possible
except through some kind of revelation. The Gentile mind had
come half into sympathy with the Jewish position that truth
was to be reached only through such enlightenment as God
had been pleased to impart through inspired men. Yet there

was general agreement with the main contention of the Greek thinkers that reason is the one criterion. Hellenistic Jews could not accept even the word of Scripture unless it was somehow reconciled with ideas that could be rationally proved.

As a result of the Gentile mission the church, while never abandoning the scriptural mode of thought, relied more and more on the methods of Greek philosophy. Paul is eager to make out that the Christian beliefs are foreshadowed in the Old Testament, and never quite feels himself on safe ground unless he can adduce a prophetic text in support of every argument. But more often than not, the text which he quotes has little relevance, and is brought in as an afterthought by way of deference to a conventional authority. His real interest is to prove that the Christian message has its sanction in man's instincts as a rational creature. He tells us, in one place, how the Gentiles, to whom the Law was denied, have yet a law written in their hearts,[6] and it is this inward law, although he affects to disparage it, which governs his thinking. He desires to set forth the gospel in such a manner that it will be recognized as in full accord with principles of reason. This came to be increasingly the aim of Christian teachers, with the result that before the second century was over Christianity was presented as a philosophy, the final outcome of the intellectual quest for God.[7] All the Christian beliefs were formulated as doctrines, stating in terms of reason what was accepted by faith.

It is true, then, that a change came over Christianity when it was set forth in theological forms. The message of Jesus had come to him by revelation, and he desired that others

[6]Rom. 2:14, 15.

[7]This is the position taken by the Apologists, though it must not be forgotten that they wrote expressly for pagan readers.

should apprehend it in like manner. "None hath known the Father but the Son, and he to whomsoever the Son will reveal him."[8] But the church ceased to rely on this immediate knowledge. It required that the truth proclaimed by Jesus should be confirmed and interpreted, and finally fell back on that authority of reason to which this world's knowledge must submit itself. The responsibility for this change has generally been laid on Paul, or at least on that Hellenistic church of which Paul was the spokesman. This may be granted in so far as theology, in its historical form, was a product of the Gentile mission, but the real change had been effected before Paul appeared on the scene. The Jerusalem teachers had sought to justify and explain their message on the ground of Scripture. Their method was different from that of their successors, but the purpose was radically the same. An appeal was made to the human intelligence. A divine message was correlated with modes of thinking which held good for this present world.

This was the decisive step which marked a turning-point in the history of the Christian religion, and it was taken very shortly after the beginning. It was not due, as we are sometimes told, to the intrusion of foreign influences, but followed as a natural consequence from the disappointment of the early hope. The church had grown aware that the coming of the Kingdom had been deferred. For an indefinite time the old order was to continue, and its requirements had now to be taken into account. Just as the church endeavoured by organizing itself to secure a place in the social framework, so it tried to fit its message into the existing forms of thought. A time would doubtless come when all truth would be understood

[8]Matt. 11:27.

immediately; the witness of the Spirit would be sufficient to itself. In some degree the people of Christ were able to walk already by the higher light. But while the present order lasted another kind of testimony was needful. Men were bound in by the earthly horizon, and the message had to be demonstrated and explained in intellectual terms. The wisdom of men is foolishness with God; His purposes cannot be defined by means of it. Yet it was necessary, as the world is now, to express the truth rationally, or it would convey no meaning to the human mind.

Here, it must be noted, we are to seek the true motive of the church's endeavour to frame a theology, whether on a scriptural or a philosophical basis. It sought to make plainer to ordinary minds what would otherwise have been utterly beyond their apprehension. Christianity, we are often told, is extremely simple, but unluckily, at some point in its history, the theologians got hold of it and entangled it in a network of doctrine. A great deal of modern religious teaching is founded on this idea that we must strip away the old theologies and so recover what is termed "the simple gospel." Now the truth is that it is not the theologies but the gospel itself which is difficult. Any one of moderate intelligence can understand a doctrine. Take for instance Justification by Faith, which seems on the face of it rather complicated, and is not very lucidly explained in the Epistle to Romans. But when it is carefully studied and put into clearer language, it is not difficult; certainly not more so than ordinary problems in mathematics or economic theory. As we learn with a little effort to feel at home with other ideas which at first are puzzling, so

Sermon on "The Worth of Doctrine".

with those of theology. Doctrine concerns the mind, and is easy; but to believe in God, to know that there is a higher world which is the real one, to accept the Cross as the true way of life—these things are extremely hard. Not one person in ten thousand can honestly affirm that he has grasped their meaning. It is the gospel itself that is difficult, so difficult that few people would make anything of it at all, if it were not for the doctrines. This was why the church put its message into theological form. It aimed at making the Christian beliefs at least partially intelligible. It recognized that if only they were offered to the mind, like ordinary objects of knowledge, the way would be opened for a higher kind of apprehension. Wise teachers from the first perceived the danger that doctrine might be mistaken for religion, and Paul complains of his Corinthians that while they excel in knowledge they have learned little of faith, hope, love. Yet the doctrines did convey some faint impression of what Christ had been, and what he had accomplished. It was possible by way of knowledge to arrive at the Christian frame of mind.

This, then, was the purpose of doctrine—to put the Christian message into rational forms so as to make it plainer to ordinary men. Living as they did under the conditions of this world they required to have the truth conveyed to them through the medium of earthly wisdom. When some one is unresponsive to a great picture or piece of music, you try to explain it to him in words. You show him, as best you can, that by certain colours or chords the artist has expressed a mood of spirit which he seeks in this way to communicate. In itself your description has little value. Painting and music have a language of their own, and the person who is ignorant of it will never take in its meaning from any laboured explanation. Yet if the right kind of feeling is present in him the commentary may serve to awaken it. He will place himself in an attitude of mind which will make it possible for the picture or the melody to speak to him for itself. It is the same with theology —for instance with the various doctrines of the Person of Christ. They describe him as the Messiah, the eternal Word, the Son of God, and these titles are all compressed statements of who he is, and what he will do for those who believe in him. Taken as they stand they do not make Christ more real to us; they might seem rather to make him more remote, substituting an abstract conception for the living Person. Yet they are helpful and indeed necessary to Christian faith. Until we form to ourselves some idea of the significance of Christ we cannot approach him with the right kind of vision. It is for this reason that Mark begins his narrative with the theological statement: "The gospel of Jesus, the Messiah, the Son of God." He is about to describe how Jesus lived and taught, but feels it necessary to impress on his readers at the very outset how they must regard this Jesus. Though to all seeming he was a man like others, he was sent by God, and his work must be considered in the light of this knowledge that it disclosed the divine purpose.

To appreciate anything great the mind must be duly prepared. You look at a star which is nothing to you but one among the myriads; but you are told of its magnitude, its infinite distance, its place in the structure of the universe. This is intellectual knowledge, but it creates in you the wonder and emotion with which you henceforth regard that star. So with theological thinking. We may say, if we please, that it is only an activity of the mind, and has no religious value. This, it must be admitted, has been true of much theology. Its main effect has been to obscure the religious interest and put in its place a merely intellectual one. But this is directly contrary to the true purpose of theology, which is to prepare the way for a more vital religion. It seeks to explain the things we believe so that we may apprehend them better and live by their power and guidance.

At the same time it cannot be affirmed too strongly that theology is not religion. The very word theology involves a contradiction. It denotes the statement of religious truth in terms of reason, and religious truth cannot be so stated. Music, it has been said, is a form of mathematics, and this is true in so far as musical sounds can be reduced to vibrations and can thus be numbered and measured. Yet with mathematics alone you would make little of a piece of music. You might be able to draw up tables of figures, exactly defining the character of the notes and the intervals between them, but this would give no indication of what is conveyed by a symphony to a musical ear. So theology is the attempt to express by reason what is given to faith, and between these two there is no doubt some correspondence, as between mathematics and music. But they are two different modes of knowledge, and the one can never be converted into the other. The rational statement will always leave out the very thing which for religion is essential. Nevertheless we are rational beings, and our instinct is to seek a rational explanation of every fact. Whatever may be its real nature we try, as we say, to "apprehend" it, which means, literally, to take hold of it. The mind is like a hand, which grasps what would otherwise be elusive, and makes it our own.

Not only so, but it is only on the plane of reason that we can communicate with each other. Thought is a kind of currency. Emotions and convictions which are personal to yourself must be changed into this denomination if you wish to impart them to your fellow men.

This parallel, however, serves to illustrate the inadequacy of theological ideas. Everything has its money value, and only on this condition can there be free interchange of goods, but the money does not in any real sense represent the thing. There is nothing in common between a banknote and a horse or a picture, although for commercial purposes it needs to be assumed that the one is the equivalent of the other. Sometimes, indeed, a man arrives at the state of mind in which a horse or a picture means nothing to him except the banknote in which it can be valued; and this is very much the condition of many theologians. They have so accustomed themselves to put the facts of religion into rational conceptions that they finally take these conceptions to be the religious facts. They offer their system of doctrine and say "this is Christianity," although the two things are just as dissimilar as a piece of stamped paper and a race-horse.

Theology, then, is not religion, and no one has perceived this more clearly than Paul, who has been accused, above all others, of turning the gospel into an intellectual code. He declared that the Kingdom of God is not meat or drink, and he insists, no less emphatically, that it is not knowledge, it is not creed or metaphysic. Spiritual things, he says, must be spiritually discerned. No formal doctrine can impart what Jesus sought to give, the trust in God, the sense of an invisible world, the peace and joy and freedom in which the new life consists.

All this was perfectly clear to the early Christian teachers. The New Testament is the fundamental book of our religion, not because it states authoritatively the doctrines to which we must assent, but because it takes us behind the doctrines. We learn from it what the gospel was, in the living experience of the first believers. When he asserts his right to be considered a true Apostle, Paul declares proudly that he had not been taught by men. His knowledge had come to him directly "by revelation of Jesus Christ."[9] Here he lays his finger on what constitutes an Apostle. The founders of the church were not the product of reasoning and instruction. The truth had been revealed to them; they were "filled with the Spirit," and their mood was one of vision and ecstasy.

None the less it was the Apostles who began that work of teaching which had its outcome in the theology of the later church. It is now recognized that our Synoptic Gospels, and in a special degree the earliest Gospel of Mark, are not mere historical narratives, as was formerly assumed, but are suffused with certain ideas which may be termed theological. This has been urged as proof that while they may preserve some genuine traditions, derived from the Apostles, they grew up for the most part out of the thinking of the later church. A view of this kind is quite unwarranted, and rests on the supposition that the church did not begin for nearly a generation to reflect on its beliefs. There is abundant evidence that the process of reflection had begun much earlier. It is apparent in the speeches attributed to Peter in the opening chapters of Acts. It is clearly indicated in various passages of Paul in which he sets his own doctrines against the background of others which

[9]Gal. 1:12.

— 134 —

he had received. The Apostles were teachers, and their teaching was bound in some measure to be theological. Proclaiming Jesus to be the Messiah they were obliged to prove that he was so, and to show what was involved in his Messiahship. The building up of a gospel tradition and the formation of a theology proceeded hand in hand.

Almost from the first, therefore, a movement began which was to have far-reaching consequences. The church had accepted its message on faith, but this was found to be insufficient, and an effort was made to bring in reason in support of faith. Beliefs which had carried with them their own evidence and forced themselves on the soul in moments of rapture were now thrown into intellectual form. The work of the Christian teacher, as Paul says, was to "persuade men."[10] His aim was to win them to the Christian faith, and he found that this must be effected by an appeal to reason. Intellectual assent came more and more to be the acknowledged basis of faith.

It is not difficult to perceive a number of causes which led to this change in the Christian attitude. For one thing, the disciples found it necessary for their own sakes to discover a rational ground for their beliefs. At first they were possessed with a glorious certitude. Jesus was the Messiah and was presently to return, and all doubt was swallowed up in the boundless ardour with which they awaited his coming. But this mood passed away, and there needed to be something else to supply its place. When the light fails you no longer see the point to which you are travelling and must think out the direction in which it lies. When you cease to take a hope for granted you try to assure yourself by discovering reasons why it cannot fail.

[10]II Cor. 5:11.

So in religion men have always fallen back on arguments to demonstrate the beliefs which at one time required no proofs. The poet, lamenting that he has lost the radiant outlook of childhood, consoles himself with the thought of "years which bring the philosophic mind." He knows, however, that his philosophy is a second-best, and this is true most of all in religion. To prove from Scripture that Jesus was the Messiah was a poor substitute for the Resurrection visions. To construct metaphysical theories of his person could not make up for the rapt experience of his invisible presence. It was not on those theories that the disciples rested their faith but on the immediate insight of which they had once been conscious. They could not but be sure of "the things they had seen and heard." Yet the memory of what had been was not enough. Increasingly they felt the need of reason to confirm and renew their faith.

Again, they were compelled to take up the new position for the sake of others. The church had now entered on its mission, and those who had known Jesus, however certain they might be in their own minds, had to make their beliefs intelligible and convincing to others. This could only be done by way of rational proof. The world at large had not shared in the early visions, and could not receive the message in the one manner whereby it could be truly apprehended. It had to be translated into the language of this world. Paul declares passionately that the wisdom of God cannot be expressed in the words which man's wisdom teaches, yet he had no choice but to employ those words.[11] For ordinary men truth has no meaning unless it can be logically proved, and this course had to be followed

[11] I Cor. 2:13.

in the presentation of the Christian message. When Paul says that he had become all things to all men that he might by any means save some, he is thinking chiefly of this rationalizing of the gospel. He argued, now as a Rabbi, now as a Greek philosopher. No one knew better than he did that the message could not be stated intellectually, but how could he preach it otherwise? Men must be approached on their own level; the message must stoop down to the doors which were open to it before it could find entrance.

But the chief cause at work in the making of Christian theology was that which has been indicated already. The church had looked for an immediate coming of the Kingdom, and the Kingdom had not come. Since the old order which had seemed on the point of closing was destined to continue, it had to be reckoned with in the preaching of the gospel, as in all else. In this world the minds of men are so constituted that all truth must be conveyed in rational form. There are other forms, which will some day come to their own. The church had relied on them in its early visions and revelations, and from time to time every man, if only for a moment, has some direct perception of the higher things. But in everyday living, under the world's conditions, all knowledge must be rational, and the Christian message, if men were to accept it, had in some way to rationalize itself. It has often been noted that Christianity never becomes a living force in any nation until it is assimilated to the national modes of thinking. The Indian or Chinaman or African must devise his own religious terms and adapt the gospel to his native culture, or it will remain outside of him. This principle has a wider and much deeper application. Prior to all the racial adjustments there is the need of adapting the divine revelation to the human mind, as it has been moulded in this world of space and time. This was the problem which faced the early church, and which found its answer in the making of a theology. By the law of their present being men apprehend all truth by their reason. Christianity had to change itself into a rational system before it could be acclimatized in the life of the world.

The process by which this was accomplished can be clearly traced in the New Testament. With each new environment in which it was placed the church altered the character of its teaching. This is commonly ascribed to the various "influences" which affected the teachers at different times, but we have to take account, perhaps in still greater measure, of a conscious adaptation. Paul deliberately became all things to all men. When he was called on to address a philosophical audience at Athens he used the ideas and language of Stoicism, and quoted from a Greek poet. It was not that the Stoic thinking had powerfully "influenced" his Christianity, it was simply because those who listened to him were accustomed to think in that manner, and he tried to convey his message in a language they would understand. At an earlier time the Apostles at Jerusalem had searched the Scriptures for proof that Jesus was the Messiah. No doubt as Jews they attached a cardinal value to the word of Scripture, but it was certainly no chance text in an ancient prophet which had convinced them of the claim of Jesus. The scriptural evidences which are adduced in the early speeches in Acts are almost all far-fetched, and this must have been apparent to the speakers themselves. They felt it necessary, however, to employ the sort of argument which carried most weight with thoughtful Jews. Since the world was to last on, the new religion connected itself with those modes of thinking which most appealed to it.

At the outset this was done by way of concession. The church was well aware that its message did not rest on scriptural or philosophical dogma, but consented, in addressing itself to the world, to make the best of the world's wisdom. At a later time the rational evidences were accepted as valid by the church itself. Reason, it was assumed, was of equal value with revelation, or might even be considered the ultimate authority. In the scholastic phrase, "fides quaerit intellectum," faith must have rational proof before it can be certain of itself. This has continued, in one form or another, to be the church's attitude. We are familiar in our day with the effort to reconcile religion with science, with philosophy, with one or another of the new social movements. One cannot but feel at times that this labour is futile and humiliating. If a man cannot believe his religion until it is certified for him by the latest experts in psychology or economics, it cannot have much inherent power. The New Testament teachers, it cannot be too strongly affirmed, never accept the rational proof as final, or even as seriously cogent. They avail themselves of everything in the thought of their time which seems to give support to their message, but always with the reservation that this is "man's wisdom." For the time being men think in this manner, according to principles which hold good for the present order, but a time is coming when everything will be different. Another world will take the place of this one, and all that we now hold certain will have lost its meaning. Faith has its real ground in the revelation of Jesus Christ.

The theology of the New Testament does not profess, therefore, to have an ultimate value. This is evident, if from nothing else, from the variety of doctrines, all conflicting with one another, which are put forward by the different writers, and sometimes by the same one. Paul, for instance, has five or six distinct theories of the meaning of the death of Christ. He is conscious that by his death Christ wrought redemption; this he discerns spiritually, as a religious fact. But when he tries to explain in rational terms why the Cross should have this power, he passes freely from one line of thought to another. It was not the aim of the New Testament writers to prove their beliefs by reason. All that they sought was to ally their message, as far as possible, with the world's manner of thinking. The church belonged to the Kingdom of God but as yet was in this world, and must be prepared to remain in it. The heavenly treasure must be put into earthly vessels.

It has been generally assumed that by the work of its teachers the new religion made a great step forward. What had previously been vague beliefs, founded on apocalyptic hopes, were placed on a firm basis of reason, and the gospel was thus able to disclose its true significance. This view, however, must be regarded as a mistaken one. It was not from a deeper insight into the message of Jesus that the early teachers were led to expound it in rational terms. Their effort was due, rather, to a weakening of the genuine religious apprehension. The day of visions and ecstasies was past, and the church was bent on maintaining itself within the present order. Faith sought to conform itself to human wisdom. The assurance once given by the Spirit was now won painfully by intellectual labour.

Men climbed by a ladder where once they had risen on wings. It may be granted indeed that when reason was thus called in to the assistance of faith, there was a rich development of religious ideas. The beliefs of the primitive church seem crude and meagre when we turn to the high speculations of Paul and the Fourth Evangelist. Yet religious thinking is not religion. It belongs to a lower plane of things and can never represent what may be given in a single flash of direct revelation. Thomas Aquinas, when he was nearing the completion of his *Sum of Theology,* had a mysterious experience, after which he broke off his mighty work. What had happened to him he would not and perhaps could not tell, but when he was urged to resume his task he said "I cannot; I have seen something which makes everything else look vain."[12] Theology at its best is only the attempt to explain religion by means that must always be inadequate, as when a blind man tries to conceive of colour in terms of sound.

So the growth of theology, which had its true origin in the teaching of the primitive church, did not mean a progress and deepening of the Christian religion. In one sense it was a confession of defeat. None the less it was one of the great achievements of the early church to lay the foundations of Christian doctrine. For one thing, if the Apostles had left nothing behind them but the memory of their visions, Christianity would soon have disappeared. A mood of rapture may mean everything to yourself, but you cannot communicate it to others. Whatever revelation it has brought you must be set forth by means of ideas, and these must in some way be demonstrated before other men will take them in. The Apostles were at pains to

[12]The incident is impressively told in Robert Bridges' *Testament of Beauty,* Book I: 485–500.

state intellectually what had come to them in vision, and by the nature of things they could do so only imperfectly. Yet the doctrinal statement was indispensable. If Christianity was to appeal to thinking men it had to be offered in a form which the mind could apprehend.

Again, it was by the creation of a theology, more even than by the tireless zeal of its missionaries, that the church made sure of its victory. It co-ordinated its message with the general thinking of the age. Men were able to respond to the new religion because there was so much in its teaching that they understood already. When Paul appeared in a foreign city he never had any difficulty in obtaining an audience. He was regarded as one of the travelling philosophical lecturers who were a familiar feature in the life of the time, and was listened to respectfully by earnest and intelligent men. This was because he met them on their own ground. He used the language which was current among Platonists and Stoics. He presented Christians truths in the light of ideas which were known, in some degree, to everybody. It made all the difference to the Christian mission that it could thus throw itself into the main current of the world's thought. Men could feel, as they. could not have done otherwise, that it had something to offer that was of real and practical concern to them. Not only so, but by bringing itself into line with other movements it was able to borrow from them much that was helpful and enriching. It has always been one of the sources of strength to our religion that it has been ready to avail itself, from time to time, of the growing results of human knowledge. Justin Martyr declared, as early as the second century, "All that has been truly thought among men belongs as a right to us Christians"; and the church has continually acted by this rule. It has justly felt that by welcoming truth from even the most unlikely quarter it is only reclaiming what is its own. When Jesus spoke of the Kingdom of God he had in mind a world of final reality on which everything must converge. All search for truth is directed in the end towards that ideal of Jesus and will help us to understand it better.

Once more, the formation of doctrine was necessary in the interests of faith itself. Paul was the greatest of the early teachers, and again and again in his Epistles he defines the purpose of his teaching as "edification," building up. It was not enough that men should be won over to the faith; they must be established in it, and this could be done only by patient instruction. They might rise now and then into ecstasy, but this could be only for a moment. There must be something stable and continuous. Faith must combine itself with ordinary thinking, and in this way alone could it become a real possession. The writer to Hebrews, enquiring into the cause of the indifference into which his readers were drifting, ascribes it chiefly to this—that they are not thinking hard enough about their religion. They are content to know the bare elements and have no desire to probe into them and explore them further. To excite them to fresh ardour he offers them a new doctrine, one which they will find difficult but which for that reason will brace the mind to strenuous effort.[13] It is a significant fact that the ages of faith have also been pre-eminently the ages of doctrine. One thinks of the New Testament age, the thirteenth century, the periods of the Reformation and of the Puritans. These were times when men passionately believed in their religion, and when

[13]Heb. 5:11; 6:3.

they also sought to explain it, with a fierce intellectual energy. In this there is nothing surprising, for the mind and the affections always react on each other. The lover of flowers wants to know botany as a science; the musician devotes himself to musical theory; the religious man cannot but be interested in theology. In itself it is only an activity of the mind, vainly striving to interpret what must always lie beyond its reach. But religion finds itself compelled to this activity, which leads, in its turn, to a deeper and more stable faith.

This was the experience of the primitive church. It began with a pure enthusiasm, arising from an immediate sense of the reality and the nearness of the Kingdom of God. It responded literally to the demand of Jesus that a man should receive the Kingdom as a little child, asking no questions, requiring no proof or argument, but simply accepting what God, in the fulness of His grace, had offered. But the Kingdom delayed its coming and the world remained; and it was this seeming failure of the Christian hope which gave rise to theology. As enthusiasm died out, men fell back on reason. Knowing that this world would continue they made use of the world's wisdom for the expression of their faith. The effort was a vain one, and doctrine has always been tentative and unsatisfying; the natural man, with his intellectual methods, cannot discern the things of the Spirit. Yet the doctrines have preserved something of the faith out of which they grew, and by their very inadequacy have kept alive the desire for a higher kind of knowledge.

CHAPTER VII

PAUL'S CONCEPTION OF THE CHURCH

Before the advent of Paul the church had taken a firm root, and had grown strong enough to alarm the Jewish authorities. In its worship, its institutions, and to some extent in its teaching, it had assumed the character which it was to bear ever afterwards. As yet, however, it was not fully conscious of itself. It had sprung up of its own accord out of the message proclaimed by Jesus, and hardly suspected that it stood for a new religion. In Paul it found a great man, and the function of a great man is to gather up in himself and bring to clear expression all that is working obscurely in the minds of others. It is sometimes alleged of Paul, as of other great men, that he made little contribution of his own. Although he was foremost in the Gentile mission he did not originate it, as has often been supposed. Although he gave organization to the church he worked on a model which had been prepared by those before him. It may be questioned whether even the theology which we associate with the name of Paul was peculiar to himself. He acknowledges his debt to the elder Apostles, and perhaps had more in common than we know with the ideas which were already current in Gentile Christianity. But through Paul the church came to realize what it was and what it was seeking for. He supplied the key not only to the later history but to the life of the church before him. We cannot rightly understand what was in the minds of the early disciples, and

— 145 —

they did not understand it themselves, except by the light of Paul.

It is unfortunate that Paul is so commonly regarded as an alien, who broke in upon the traditions of the church. To many writers it has seemed an almost inexplicable problem that such a man should have come to ally himself with a group which at every point was so little in sympathy with him. The truth is, however, that Paul was a child of the primitive church. When he became a Christian it had been only a short time in existence—no more, perhaps, than a few months or a year— and still was essentially the same as it had been at first. He learned his Christianity from the immediate disciples of Jesus. He was baptized into the primitive community, and worked as one of its accredited teachers. Luke has been sternly criticized for making Jerusalem the centre from which Paul went forth on his several missions, and to which he continued to feel himself responsible. This, we are told, is a palpable misrepresentation, and distorts the whole course of the early history. But while Luke's account may in some ways be artificial, he was acquainted with the facts, and there is no reason to doubt his main assumption. Paul belonged to the primitive community, and although he may not have kept strictly under its supervision he never ceased to regard himself as one of its teachers. Travelling, as he did, into many distant countries he carried with him the spirit and the motives of the brotherhood in Jerusalem.

Through Paul, therefore, we obtain our best insight into the mind of the primitive church. The earlier disciples had never reflected on the nature of the community which had formed under their leadership. If they had sought to describe it they would doubtless have done so in quite different terms from Paul. It is only too evident that in some respects they failed to perceive the true character of the enterprise in which they were engaged, and placed themselves in opposition to Paul. Yet with his gift of ignoring side-issues and penetrating to the heart of every subject, he grasped the real meaning of what his fellow-labourers were doing unconsciously. For the first time he raised the question: "What is this church of which we Apostles are servants?" By his answer he made the church aware of its destiny, and started it on its historical task.

There might seem, at first sight, to be two aspects of Paul's thinking, in sharp contradiction to each other. On the one hand, he is an individualist. Religion, as he conceives it, is a personal relation between the soul and Christ. It rests on the principle of faith, and faith, as he sees it, has no worth or meaning unless it is your own faith. Paul can say of himself that he did not learn his gospel from men, neither was he taught it;[1] he had received it directly from Christ, and for that reason could depend on it with utter certainty. He knows Christ as "my Lord, who loved me and gave himself for me."[2] He is conscious of an immediate union between his soul and Christ, so that he can declare, "I live, yet not I, but Christ lives in me." His aim, therefore, is to bring his converts into that personal fellowship with Christ which he himself has experienced. Christ has made them free, and they are not to put themselves under bondage to men. They are to feel that they have been individually chosen by the grace of God. Their knowledge of God is to be their own, given to them immedi-

[1]Gal. 1:12.　　　　　　　　[2]Gal. 1:20.

Paul's emphasis on the Christian fellowship —

ately by the indwelling Spirit. This personal note is everywhere present in Paul's teaching, and in all times when religion has become formal and external men have gone back to Paul. He has enabled them to shake themselves free from all human authority, and recover the sense that they may approach God in their own right as His children. Paul may be justly regarded as the very foremost of all the soldiers of liberty.

On the other hand, Paul was an ecclesiastic, the first Christian leader known to us to whom this name may properly be applied. The thought of the church is constantly in his mind, and apparently had been so from the outset. When he became a Christian his first action was to have himself baptized as a member of the church. Wherever he went, in the course of his missionary labours, his object was to form a community, representing in its own locality the one indissoluble church of Christ. We read in the book of Acts how Philip, as he journeyed along a desert coast, fell in with an Ethiopian and sent him back to his native land as a Christian.[3] In the history of Paul there is no similar episode. Wherever he made a convert his first care was to associate him with a community. A Christian who stood all by himself was unthinkable to Paul. Christianity, to his mind, implied membership in the church, and the act of baptism by which a man entered on the new life in the Spirit was at the same time his incorporation in the brotherhood. On one occasion Paul requires that an unworthy member should be excommunicated, and tells how this must be done at a special meeting, solemnly convened. He takes for granted that the man who is thus renounced by the community is in that moment "delivered over to Satan." He has lost

[3]Acts 8:26 f.

his part in the Christian salvation and is thrown back to the prince of this world, who will duly punish him as a deserter, now recaptured.[4] So for Paul the Christian religion is inseparable from the church, and his letters are addressed to churches and deal for the most part with the principles of church conduct and teaching. When the author of the Pastoral Epistles desires at a later time to formulate the necessary rules of church order, he attributes his work to Paul. This was the Apostle who stood out, for all Christians afterwards, as the typical ecclesiastic. Above all others he had concerned himself with the interests of the church, and his directions were to be taken as authoritative.

It is difficult to reconcile these two attitudes which are equally characteristic of Paul. How could the Apostle of individual freedom be likewise the champion of the church, which aims at limiting and controlling that freedom? Paul himself, however, is unconscious of any contradiction, and when his thought is viewed as a whole we can recognize that he is fully consistent. If there is any contradiction it must be found, not in the mind of Paul, but in nature itself. In a previous discussion of the communal idea in Christianity we had occasion to note that what is called an individual is only a separate member of a group or species.[5] To be sure, the individual qualities are all-important, and constitute the identity of the given plant or animal or man. But they are variations of the type, and before we can make anything of the separate creature we must place it within the type to which it belongs. In accordance with this law the people of Christ became a community. They realized from the first that they did not stand separate but all

[4]I Cor. 5:1 f.   [5]See Chapter III.

embodied that new type of humanity which had appeared in the world through Christ. If each of them was to develop his own Christian life they must all be bound together in a brotherhood. With Paul this sense of community was peculiarly strong. He was possessed with the idea of a universal scope and value in the work of Christ. "As in Adam all die, even so in Christ shall all be made alive."[6] The one redemption had availed for all men; it had made possible the renewal of all earthly nature. Christ had come to create a new race of men, and each of his disciples must be mindful that what he has received from Christ he shares with others, who have undergone the same change. It follows that no man can become a Christian unless he is included in the community. His Christianity implies that he is one of the new race, apart from which he cannot fulfil his individual Christian life.

There is therefore no conflict between Paul's demand for a personal faith and his other demand for membership in the church. If a man desires to be in the fullest sense himself, he does not attain this end by retiring into solitude. His common humanity is part of himself, by far the greater part of it, and he must exercise and develop it in intercourse with his fellow men. By shutting himself off he does not gain in personality but only shrivels into an ego which is worthless to himself and to everybody. The Christian man, likewise, if he would possess an individual faith, must make himself one with the Christian fellowship. By separating himself he loses all contact with Christ, who is present in him individually because he is present in the whole community of believers.

There is no contradiction between the personal faith of Paul

[6] I Cor. 15:22.

and his devotion to the church. Neither are we to think of them as two different strands which happened to be woven together in his religion. An artist may also be an ardent patriot, and his love of country will probably reflect itself in his art, but between art and patriotism there is no intrinsic connection. So it has been held that Paul combined two interests which had little to do with each other. He was a saint or mystic who was also a born administrator, and with this practical side of his nature was zealous in the service of the church. But the more we examine his thought the more we perceive that his devotion to the church was a vital element in his personal religion; the two interests were fundamentally one and the same. It was because he sought an inward fellowship with Christ that he felt the need of union with the Christian society. This attitude of Paul has had its counterpart in that of many Christian leaders in later times. The term "ecclesiastic" is often used disparagingly, to denote the church politician whose whole concern is with the externals and mere machinery of religion. Yet the truly great ecclesiastics, men like Athanasius, Augustine, Bernard, Calvin, Wesley have been first of all great Christians. It was their insight into the principles of Christianity which made them eager to build up the Christian community. So with ordinary men and women, almost as a general rule, the religious spirit goes hand in hand with loyalty to the church. There always have been those who stood aloof from the church, claiming that they could serve God better in the privacy of their own souls. It may be doubted, however (if a judgment can be formed from outward tokens), whether this isolated religion is very deep or sincere. The Christians of whom we can be certain that their lives are hid with Christ in

God are invariably to be found within the church. They may appear sometimes to attach undue importance to mere details of church custom and ordinance. They lay themselves open, not always unjustly, to the charge of confusing the inward with the outward. Yet the formal devotion does, in some indefinable way,,blend with the spiritual one and deepen it. Love for the community is hardly•to be distinguished from the love of Christ.

Paul, then, is fully conscious of the bond between the church and the inner Christian life. Reference has been made to the Pastoral Epistles, in which ecclesiastical questions are discussed from what is conceived to be the Pauline point of view. On various grounds it is more than probable that those Epistles, though based to some extent on Pauline material, are not the genuine work of Paul; and the weightiest argument is this— that the writer has missed the intangible and yet vital element in Paul's conception of the church. He looks at it in its external aspect as the society which maintains the Christian faith and which therefore must be safeguarded and wisely administered. For Paul himself it is an essential factor in the Christian faith. It is the necessary means whereby the believer participates in the Spirit, and enters into living fellowship with Christ. Paul has indeed much to say about the practical duties of the church, and the methods by which it can perform them more effectually. But his chief concern is always with its inward significance. While it exists as an ordered society, its function is to assist its individual members in that new life which has come to them through Christ. One of the characteristic words of Paul is "communion" (*koinonia*), a word which is dif-

Paul's Conception of the Church

ficult to explain, because it always carries with it a twofold meaning. Christians have communion with Christ and also with one another; and these two kinds of fellowship are bound together, and are ultimately the same. The very meaning of •the church, as Paul understands it, is that it is a union of the brethren through which we enter into union with Christ himself.

This is an idea which is presented in various ways throughout Paul's Epistles, but his thought is expressed most clearly by means of two striking images. Like most of Paul's images they are not entirely metaphorical, but are meant rather to be statements in concrete language of spiritual facts.

On the one hand, Paul thinks of the church as the Body of Christ. He set out, apparently, by using this idea as little more than an illustration. His Corinthian converts were making invidious distinctions between the different spiritual gifts, attaching superior value to such endowments as prophecy and speaking with tongues, which bore the evident stamp of a supernatural power. He declares that all activities which further the well-being of the church are due to the Spirit, and that all are equally noble and necessary. The church, he says, is like the human body, which consists of many members, each one with its special function, while all are dependent on one another and operate in harmony. An injury to one is felt by all; the service of one organ may seem inferior to that of another, and yet if it were lacking the whole body would suffer.[7] The analogy was one which had often been used in ancient thought, particularly with reference to the state, which cannot hold together unless all ranks and classes are willing to co-

[7] I Cor. 12:12 f.

— 153 —

operate, each in the place assigned to it. Paul, however, gave a new and profound application to the familiar image. He was the first to apprehend a great principle which has since proved infinitely fruitful in almost every department of knowledge—the principle of unity in difference. In mere uniformity there can be no true unity. A block of sandstone, made up of millions of identical grains, is not really one. The grains are not united but only crushed together, and when they are separated each of them remains what it was before. A plant, with its root and stem and leaves and flower, is a unity; because the parts are different they are all interwoven and serve the indivisible life of the plant. Most of all the human body is the perfection of unity. It consists of thousands of parts which by their difference minister to each other, and blend in the one personality which thinks and wills.

Paul desires that the church should be one as the body is one. He is concerned immediately with the spiritual gifts which are diverse and yet work in harmony; but it cannot be doubted that he would have passed a similar judgment on differences of church order and practice and (doctrine.) He does so, at least by implication, in an earlier chapter of this same Epistle to the Corinthians.[8] They had broken into parties, calling themselves by the names of leaders, Paul, Apollos, Cephas, who had presented the gospel in different ways. He points out that each leader had made his own contribution to the common cause. Christ is not divided. He makes use of many instruments, and if they are to help on his purpose they need to be different. The varying types of teaching are all in harmony, in so far as each of them is necessary for the full apprehension of the one truth.

[8] I Cor. 3.

In his first intention, then, Paul aimed at showing that the church is an organism, all the more closely knit together because of its diversities. But his conception of the Body of Christ came to possess a much deeper import for his thinking. The body is one because it is pervaded in all its parts by one life-giving principle; what is it that animates the church and holds it together? It can be nothing else than Christ himself, who dwells in the church and uses it in his service. When he lived on earth he manifested himself in a body, and now he has undergone a new incarnation. The church, in a sense, is Christ himself, still visibly present in the world. This idea is most fully set forth in the Epistle to the Ephesians, the authenticity of which has sometimes been denied, on grounds which cannot be deemed adequate. That it represents the view of Paul is indubitable, because its teaching is plainly suggested in other Epistles. In the argument of Ephesians an almost literal meaning is attached to the idea of the Body of Christ. As the soul animates the body, so Christ abides in his church. Each Christian, in virtue of his place in the community, is related to Christ and partakes of his divine life. He can say, as Paul says of himself: "I live, yet not I, but Christ lives in me." Paul's doctrine of the church is thus an essential part of his mysticism. He believes that every Christian has a personal fellowship with Christ and is thus set free from all authority of men. Yet he holds that this personal fellowship is mediated by the Christian community. According as he is a living member of the church the believer has part in Christ himself, who is the vital principle of the body in which he dwells.

Paul expresses his thought from another side by his conception of the church as the earthly counterpart of the higher

The Nature of the Early Church

spiritual order. This idea may be said to underlie all the Epistles, but it is stated most explicitly in a verse of Philippians: "our citizenship is in heaven."[9] Here again we have much more than a vivid and impressive metaphor. Paul thinks of the church as belonging to the heavenly world. To all appearance it is a society like others, made up for the most part of very ordinary men and women; "Few who are noble or wise or mighty have been called."[10] But they have identified themselves with the Kingdom of God. Living in the present world, their true affinities are with a world that lies beyond. A nation may be represented in a foreign country by a handful of traders or soldiers, who mingle with the people around them and adapt themselves to the alien modes of living. Yet their interests are in the distant land from which they came. In times of danger they display their native flag, and feel safe under its protection. Paul has this analogy in his mind and wishes it to be taken literally. The church is placed on earth as an outpost of the heavenly world. Its members are submissive to the present order, but owe their allegiance to another. This is the suggestion which lies always in the background when Paul speaks of "the Lord." Christians are to remind themselves by the use of this name that they belong to a realm in which Christ is sovereign. By their baptism into his church they have transferred their loyalty, and have their citizenship in heaven.

Reason for Persecution

We have here to find the true reason why Christianity, almost from the beginning, was subject to persecution. Pagan society in the early centuries knew little of the Christian teaching, but it was obscurely aware that the followers of Christ, while living in the midst of it, were a foreign people. "These

[9]Phil. 3:20.   [10]I Cor. 1:26.

all do contrary to the decrees of Cæsar, saying that there is another king, one Jesus."[11] This judgment was wrong in so far as it condemned the church as a political organization, bent on the destruction of the existing government. Yet it could find its justification in Paul's conception of the nature of the church. He believed, in no mere figurative sense, that it was the advance guard of a different power from that which the world acknowledged. Its members had released themselves from their old allegiance and embraced a new citizenship. This, for Paul, was the very purpose of the church—to stand in this world for that other order of things which is realized in heaven.

From all this it follows that Paul insists on the separateness of the church. This side of his teaching, as we know from his own admission, had caused perplexity among his converts. He had written, "Come out from among them and be ye separate";[12] and they had taken this to mean that they were to have no contact with the world and were to form themselves into some kind of hermit community. They had protested that life under these conditions would be impossible. Paul takes care to assure them that they had mistaken his meaning. So long as this world existed the Christians were to take their part in it, and if they held aloof from their neighbours it must be only from those who were living in notorious sin.[13] None the less he impresses on them that they were a people apart. While sharing in the ordinary life of the city they were to avoid everything that might savour of idolatry. They were to feel that their fellow-Christians were closer to them than others,

[11]Acts 17:7.   [12]II Cor. 6:17.   [13]I Cor. 5:9 f.

and had a special claim on them. All disputes that might arise within the society were to be settled by arbiters of its own appointment, without recourse to the regular law-courts.[14] This injunction is highly significant. Paul had an excessive regard for Roman justice, and believed that in any conflict of interests it was sure to give an impartial decision. Again and again he admonishes his readers to trust the laws and those who administered them, and in this trust he himself made his fatal appeal to Cæsar. Yet he requires that the church, even in worldly matters, should be independent of all outside authority. Christians must never forget that they were citizens of another world.

It is from this point of view that Paul's whole work as a missionary should be understood. His outlook was far wider than that of the primitive disciples, but he never ceased to be faithful to the original conception of the church. It was the community which would inherit the Kingdom. The Judgment was at hand, and the people of Christ would be rescued from the perishing world and would be set apart for eternal life. To a great extent Paul had abandoned this early apocalyptic view. He thought of salvation, not as something reserved for the future, but as given now, in the act of faith. But his object was still to bring men into the holy community and so effect their rescue from this world of perdition. In the view of many people today, the chief value of the church is its leavening influence. Only a small minority may actually belong to it, but they exercise a moral leadership which is everywhere acknowledged. The church is the guardian of all higher standards; it ensures that law should be grounded in right principles, that

[14] I Cor. 6:1 f.

business should be conducted honestly, that the strong should protect the weak, that customs should be seemly and humane. Not so much for its own sake as for this uplifting effect on the general life, the church must be preserved.

Modern Motive of Missions

A similar judgment is applied to Christian missions. No one, we are told, can seriously believe that the vast populations of India, Japan, China will ever become Christian, and this, perhaps, is not altogether desirable. Missionary effort, in so far as its aim is purely religious, is largely wasted. Its true value consists in its civilizing influence. It serves to instil into backward races something of the morality which has grown out of our religion. It leads to the establishment of schools, hospitals, all the helpful institutions which are found in Christian lands. The real benefits of missions are of this indirect kind. Their religious success may be very limited but this does not greatly matter, so long as they raise the general level of culture and imbue non-Christian peoples with some of the beneficent ideas of Christianity.

Much may be said for this conception of the church as a society which diffuses a better spirit through the world around it, even though it does not actually change men into Christians. This, however, was not the conception of Paul. He thought of the church as standing by itself, over against the world, and his one aim as a missionary was to draw men out of the world into the church. There is no sign that he ever had any desire to elevate and improve the heathen society. No charge, indeed, has been so often and so vehemently urged against him as that he never protested against prevailing evils—slavery, the exploitation of subject races, unjust distribution of wealth, the degrading sports of the amphitheatre. Such things must have

This was not Paul's

been utterly repugnant to him, but apparently he never felt himself called on to denounce them. If he had contemplated nothing more than to improve conditions in the world of the first century he would certainly never have undertaken his mission. All the evils as he saw them were inherent in the old order, and were bound to continue, in one form or another, so long as it lasted. Even if it had been possible for him to amend existing institutions it is doubtful whether he would have tried to do so. He would have reasoned that the world, however it was ameliorated, still would be the world. It was intrinsically wrong, and any attempt to make it superficially better would serve only to blind men's eyes to its real nature. The evils of the world must be left as they were. They were less dangerous if they could be plainly seen as part of an order which was wholly contrary to the will of God. Nothing would suffice but that men should be rescued out of this world which was doomed to destruction. So the church, in Paul's view, was not meant to be a leaven or an influence, existing for the sake of human society at large. It represented the higher order of things, and men were to be brought into it. While they remained outside of it, however they might be elevated by some of its gifts to them, it availed them nothing. What they required was the new life which only Christ could bestow on those who were in living fellowship with him through his church.

This attitude of Paul is undoubtedly open to criticism. It has been the glory of the church in past ages, and more than ever in our own, that it has done so much for those who had no part in it, and who often kept deliberately aloof. It has been in the forefront of every battle for liberty, for the relief of pain and poverty, for the humanizing of material and social conditions. Without any direct intention of making men Christians it has ministered to them simply as men, and in so doing it has surely fulfilled the law of Christ. But Paul, in his intense conviction that Christian faith was the one supreme interest, was impatient of all lower ones, and it was this which gave him power to achieve his great mission. The thought was always present to him that the time was short, and that the Kingdom was ready to break in. Men must be saved from this world, which even now was crumbling under their feet, and throw in their lot with the new order. Paul worked at fever heat under the stress of this conviction that he must build up the church as the one city of refuge for mankind.

It has been often pointed out that in his insistence on the separateness of the church he tends to be narrow and exclusive. The virtue which he prizes most is "love of the brethren." He commonly speaks of Christians as "the saints," using this term in its primary meaning of those who are separated from others. In his various accounts of moral duties he has chiefly the life of the community in his mind. Again and again he might seem to restrict the love of Christ to the church, which he purchased with his own blood. It may indeed be granted that we do not find in Paul that all-embracing humanity which attracts us in the teaching of Jesus, to whom God is the Father of all men, sending down His rain and sunshine on the evil and the good alike; but it would be wrong to compare his exclusiveness to that of small-minded sects which confine their sympathies wholly to their own group, and are hardly aware of the people outside of it. He had probably seen more of the world than any other man of his time. He possessed, almost in an excessive

degree, the responsive temper which enabled him to become
all things to all men. We do not rightly understand his attitude unless we allow for two objects which he had in view
when he called on the church to be separate. On the one hand,
he wishes to impress on the community that while here in the
world it must be always on its guard. Its members must never
be forgetful of their high calling. However they mix with
others they must carry with them their own motives and standards; they must think of Christ as their one Master. There is
a sense in which every high-minded man must be exclusive.
He has something which he holds sacred, and at a certain
point draws a boundary between himself and the crowd. In
the same manner the church must be exclusive. Whatever may
be its other interests the religious one is paramount, and if
this is to be kept secure its members must fence themselves off
from much that pertains to the common life. More than once
Paul compares the church to a temple, and in ancient times a
temple stood in a walled enclosure, dividing it from the noise
and business of the city. The church was the temple of the
living God, and must separate itself.

But Paul also desires this separateness for the sake of the
world itself. The aim of his mission was to draw men out of
the world into the church, and they could not be so drawn unless they could clearly perceive that the church was different.
In a number of passages in his letters Paul shows himself anxious, it might seem unduly so, about the world's opinion. The
church must expose itself to no ridicule or scandal. It must be
careful that its members live up to their profession. It must
forbid them to take part in customs and festivities which might
bring them too closely into contact with their pagan surround-

ings. This solicitude for the good name of the church was natural, and was particularly necessary in a time when there were enemies on every side, eager to find some pretext for criticism and slander. But Paul has evidently a further object. He is intent on winning men to his cause, and knows that his labour will go for nothing unless the church stands out from ordinary society. It represents a higher order of things, and this must be made apparent even to the most unthinking. In all that they know of the Christians they must be brought to see that this community does not belong to their world. Paul was well aware that by thus separating itself the church would incur dislike and persecution, for men resent everything that offends the custom of the herd. But he knew that this very aloofness of the church would be its power. The world would find itself confronted with something totally different from itself, and thereby would be attracted. Every city in that age was full of guilds and clubs and friendly societies, and if the church appeared to be merely one of them, it would hardly be worth notice. Men must see at once that it was a new kind of association. The stranger, Paul says, as he looks in upon your meeting, "will be convinced by all and judged by all; the secrets of his heart will be made manifest, and falling down on his face he will worship God, and will report that God is in you of a truth."[15]

Paul insists, then, that the church should be separate, in the sense that it should keep itself distinct from the surrounding life of paganism. Men were to know from its whole attitude and from the character of its members that it belonged to an-

[15] I Cor. 14:24, 25.

other order. At the same time he recognized, apparently from the first, that it must adjust itself to the present age. If it were to answer its purpose as an outpost of the Kingdom it must be willing to submit, for the time being, to the alien conditions. Paul could see this more clearly than the elder Apostles, for although he was a child of the primitive church he had been "born out of due time."[16] He was not confused with memories of the first ecstatic days when the Kingdom seemed already to be breaking in. From the outset of his Christian career he had taken the present order for granted and allowed a place for it in his beliefs. To be sure he shared in the expectation that the end was near, and was confident that he himself would live to witness it; but he counted on many years of activity which were still at his disposal. This is evident from the grandiose plan on which he conducted his mission. He would visit personally all the provinces of the Roman empire, first in the East and then in the West, and establish in each of them at least one community which would be a centre of light for the region round about it. In this manner he would fulfil his intention of preaching the gospel to the whole world.[17] Latterly he seems to have lost his early confidence. As the result, perhaps, of a terrible experience at Ephesus, when he lay for a time under sentence of death,[18] he realized that he would not live to see the Lord's coming. This, however, involved no essential change in his outlook. He became aware that the world would last longer than he had reckoned on, but he had already allowed for its continuance during a space of years.

It was thus clear to Paul that the church must not break

[16]I Cor. 15:8.
[17]This plan is outlined by Paul himself in Rom. 15:18–24.
[18]II Cor. 1:8–10. Also I Cor. 15:32.

with the world. Remaining separate it had yet to take account of the earthly environment, and not only avoid any quarrel with it but use it, as far as possible, for the furtherance of its work. The main object of all the Epistles is to advise the churches on difficulties that have arisen from their twofold relation to the higher order and the earthly one. Paul writes with a view only to the short interval which has still to elapse before the advent of the Kingdom. This interval has now extended to nearly twenty centuries, but Paul faced his problem with such an insight into its nature that his counsels have always remained valid. He may be justly regarded as the great architect of the church. It stands today, in almost everything that concerns its relation to the world, much as we see it in the design of Paul.

The Epistles deal with a large variety of practical questions; each community had difficulties of its own, and Paul examines them carefully, and sometimes in much detail. It might have been expected that his conclusions would be now of little interest, since the matters submitted to him were often local and trivial, and were bound up with old-world conditions which have long ceased to exist. But it was the rare gift of Paul to see the general in the particular. However insignificant may be the case before him he pierces at once to the principle involved in it, and his judgments are therefore of lasting value. These judgments, moreover, are based on certain firm convictions which he had no doubt reached after much pondering on the necessary relations between the church and the world.

He is convinced, for one thing, that the church must constitute itself as an orderly society. Enthusiasm is desirable, and

Paul possessed it in the fullest measure. He could speak in
tongues more than them all; he knew what it was to be caught
up into the third heaven. But with his capacity for rapture
Paul had also the mind of a statesman. Confusion of any kind
was abhorrent to him, and he believed that it was so to God.
Everything must be done "decently and in order." He was
averse, also, to mere fanaticism. He conceives of the Christian
life as a race in which the prize will go to him that has staying
power, and has disciplined himself, and is "temperate in all
things." The true gifts of the Spirit are those which manifest
themselves, not in frenzied outbursts, but in practical service
and a constant fellowship with God. Love, which is stedfast
and can bear up through all discouragements, is the greatest of
the spiritual gifts. But Paul's endeavour to organize the church
was not due simply to his instinct for order and reality. He saw
that nothing enduring could be made out of mere religious
fervour, and the church must prepare itself to endure. The
return of Christ had been delayed, and the present world was
to last on. If the church were not to disappear it must somehow come to terms with the world's conditions. It must take
the form of a regular society, able to hold its own in the social
structure of the time.

Paul therefore made it his aim to impose some kind of system on his churches. He laid down rules for the conduct of
worship, for works of beneficence, for communal and family
relations. He provided each group with a staff of officers, and
during his absences kept in touch with it through his assistants
and by means of letters. The churches were widely scattered,
and were all jealous of their independence, but he tried to
draw them together. It is possible that in the latter part of his

career there floated before his mind the idea of a federation, under the presidency of Jerusalem. Something of this kind seems to be indicated by that scheme for a collection, of which we hear so much in the later Epistles. In any case, by the practical effort to enlist them all in a common enterprise he sought to awaken in his churches a sense of their solidarity. Their ideal unity as the church of Christ was to manifest itself in active co-operation. So in every way Paul set himself deliberately to build up and regulate his communities, and behind all his action we can trace one governing motive. While he thought of the church as a spiritual brotherhood, reflecting the higher order, he perceived that here on earth it must ally itself with the existing order. If it were to survive as the community of the Kingdom, it must also take the form of an organization, fitted to the requirements of this world.

Along with this endeavour to devise rule and system, Paul is anxious, in every way he can think of, to promote friendliness between the church and the world it lives in. Christians in the earlier time had tried to break away from everything that pertained to the present order, which was nearing its end. Paul seeks to bring them back to realities. He impresses on them that they must take their part, as far as conscience permits them, in the ordinary activities. They are to work for their living in the occupations they have been used to follow. If they are slaves they are to obey their masters, although knowing that they have become free men in Christ. Instead of rebelling against existing laws and institutions they must be doubly careful to respect them, and to do so willingly.

It is in this connection that we must understand Paul's attitude to women, which has laid him open to so much misconception in later times. He has been accused of thinking of women disparagingly and going out of his way to lay restrictions on them; but this is certainly far from the truth. He declares that in Christ there is neither male nor female; all human beings are now on an equal footing, and have the same worth in the sight of God. He found perhaps his most valued helpers among women. He gave a place to them in the ministry of the church, recognizing their peculiar gifts as teachers, comforters, agents of charity. It may truly be said that he was one of the great pioneers in the emancipation of women; and this, indeed, is the very reason why he is led at times to speak of them with apparent harshness. He had taught them that they were free, with the result that some of them were inclined to abuse their new-found liberty. For his own part, we can well believe, Paul would not have interfered, but he had to take account of ancient sentiment, especially in Gentile countries, which required a strict decorum on the part of women. Nothing could be more harmful to the church than to have it supposed that its women were forward and domineering, and Paul insists that at least in the formal meetings to which strangers were freely admitted, they should keep in the background, and wear the customary veil. In this, as in other things, he seeks to conciliate the world's opinion. The church must conform its practice to that of ordinary society. It must not wilfully offend the prevailing sentiment, even when this was different from its own. If it was to make its home in the world and win it over, it must be friendly and accommodating.

Paul enforces this rule with a special emphasis whenever he deals with the relation of Christians to the civil power. We come here to a large question which will call for discussion in a separate chapter, but at present it will be enough to note that Paul desires his converts to behave as good citizens. They must submit to the laws of the state, pay all dues and taxes, honour the emperor, and the rulers and magistrates under him. These counsels were obviously wise, in view of the position of the church in the first century. There was much in its teaching that seemed subversive of the established order, and it was notoriously to blame for the breaking up of many families. The riots which interfered from time to time with Paul's own mission were not entirely due to the ignorance of the mob, incited by hostile Jews and agitators. Pagan society had a real case against the church, as representing a dangerous movement which needed to be suppressed before it had gone too far. The situation was aggravated by hotheaded elements in the church itself. When the city of Rome was burned down in 64 A.D. the rumour gained ground that it was the Christians who started the fire. Almost certainly this was due to nothing else than the natural instinct to find a scapegoat for every disaster, but it is significant that in this instance suspicion fell on the Christians. It was known that they looked for the end of the world, and that there were some who held this belief in a fanatical form. Might it not be that they had tried to hasten the end?

We can understand, then, why Paul enjoins obedience to law and authority. He saw that a terrible menace hung over the church, and could be averted only by the utmost circumspection on the part of its members. But this prudential motive is combined for Paul with a much deeper one. He is alive to the fact that although the church is not of the world it must live alongside of it. The end is not to come immediately, and meanwhile the community of the Kingdom must accept the present order. In the teaching of Paul there is much that looks like compromise, and it has been inferred that while he was a Christian enthusiast he was also a shrewd politician, and perhaps something of a timeserver. Charges of this kind were brought against him in his lifetime, and we know from his letters that he bitterly resented them. He was well aware of his true motives. He perceived that if the church was to carry on its task it must come to some agreement with the earthly order, which was evidently to continue, no one could tell how long. Only on this condition could it maintain itself and fulfil its purpose. If it stood wholly apart it would always remain foreign, and those who might have welcomed its message would be repelled. It must find some common ground with the world before the world would accept it.

Paul speaks of himself in one passage as "a wise master-builder" who has planned the foundation of an edifice which those who followed him must complete worthily, with materials which will bear the test of time.[19] Every one would now acknowledge that he has rightly described his work. The church that rose up in the ages that succeeded him was built, in all essentials, according to his plan. He transformed the primitive group of Christians into a great society, which even before his death was spreading itself over the whole extent of the Roman empire. He worked deliberately on a principle without which this vast expansion would never have been possible. While his predecessors had clung to the belief that the world was all but finished, and had sought to guard the church

[19]I Cor. 3:10.

from all contact with it, Paul accepted the world and aimed at adapting the church to its conditions. The primitive brotherhood became in his hands an organization, availing itself of methods and instruments which were frankly borrowed from the world's order. Nevertheless for Paul, as for the earlier Apostles, the church was separate. It was the fellowship of the saints, and stood, amidst the things of time, for the Kingdom of God. "We have died to sin and live unto righteousness." "Our citizenship is in heaven." Christians are to be reconciled to the world they live in, and yet be conscious always of their higher calling. Outwardly they must conform to this passing world, while in their inner being they are set apart as the people of Christ. Paul has so blended these two ideas that they do not conflict, but illuminate and support each other, and it is this which gives permanent value to his teaching on the church.

CHAPTER VIII

THE ETHICAL TASK OF THE CHURCH

To outside observers the church in the primitive days was a group of enthusiasts, intoxicated for the moment with a fanatical hope which would soon prove an illusion. The wisest of contemporary Jews was the Rabbi Gamaliel, whose speech at the Council is recorded in the book of Acts. "I say unto you, Refrain from these men and let them alone; for if this work be of men it will come to nought, but if it be of God ye cannot overthrow it."[1] Gamaliel spoke in guarded fashion, but the idea in his mind is not hard to guess. The work, as he saw it, was of men—one of the ignorant excitements of which he had known many in his time. They had all run their day and been forgotten, and the Council would be foolish to view the matter seriously and perhaps give impetus, by harsh measures, to a movement which would die down in natural course if it were only let alone. This was a sensible attitude, and we still adopt it in face of the new cults and sensations which are constantly bubbling to the surface. They irritate us while they last, but we try to keep our temper and let them fizz themselves out. We can be confident that nothing unsubstantial will trouble us for long.

From the first, however, Christianity was more than an excitement, inspired by wild apocalyptic hopes. Jesus had indeed proclaimed the Kingdom of God, but he had also revealed the

[1]Acts 5:38.

will of God, as it would be done in the Kingdom. He had required of his followers that they should conduct their lives
according to that higher pattern, and after his death they had
made it their aim to observe his precepts. The earliest name
by which they called their movement was "the Way," the new
manner of life which had been prescribed by Jesus. Their hope
for the Kingdom was combined with a moral .activity, and
those who looked only to what seemed fanatical in the new
beliefs did not allow for this other element. The enthusiasm
died down, as might have been expected, but the Christian
community was securely anchored to that new righteousness
which had been set forth in the Sermon on the Mount.

In all ages this has been the permanent thing in our religion.
Theologies have succeeded each other, ritual has passed
through many phases, countless sects have arisen, so different
in character that it is sometimes hard to distinguish their
family likeness. But the Christian ethic has always remained
substantially the same. The mediæval saints had many fancies
which now appear strange to us, but they practised the Christian virtues, just as we understand them now. A Roman Catho-
lic and a Quaker may seem to be at opposite poles in their
worship, but when you ask their judgment on purely moral
questions, they answer the same way. Sometimes it is argued
that morality has nothing to do with religion, and remains constant, by its own nature, under all forms of belief. This, however, is not true. The old pagan idea of a good man was
radically different from the Christian one, and the chief difficulty of the early missionaries was not so much to enforce
their doctrines as to change the moral attitude. Even to noble
pagans like Marcus Aurelius the behaviour of the Christians

appeared foolish or positively wicked.[2] Jesus did not take over the generally accepted ethic but for the most part reversed it, and it was this new morality which impressed itself on his followers, and became the unchanging element in their religion.

The conclusion has often been drawn that the only thing in Christianity which really matters is its ethic. "For forms of faith let fools and bigots fight, He can't be wrong whose life is in the right." A view of this kind has grown increasingly common in our time. We are told that the religion of Jesus was little more than a sheath for the protection of certain moral principles. When these have been secured, the sheath may be thrown away, and our one task now is to give practical effect to those conceptions of justice, kindness, human equality which Jesus brought into the world. He belonged to an ancient time and an eminently religious nation, so it is not surprising that he associated his ethic with the customary beliefs about God. But his vital interest was in moral action, and we can still remain Christians, in the essential meaning of the term, although we dispense with the old beliefs, which have now become a burden.

This, however, is a complete misunderstanding of the purpose of Jesus. His sayings, to be sure, are concerned mostly with the moral and social life, but when we consider them more deeply they are bound up inseparably with his religion. Morality was not his vital interest. On the contrary, he regarded it only as a means towards an end. If one were asked to select the central saying of Jesus, which supplies the key to all the others, it might be found in the verse of the Sermon on

[2]He sees nothing in the death of the martyrs but a "stupid obstinacy."

the Mount, "that ye may be the children of your Father who is in heaven."[3] The motive of all right action is here definitely stated, and it is one which distinguishes the Christian type of morality from all others. Why should I act in the manner I call right? This is the primary moral question, and the answer given to it must always determine the character of an ethical code. Sometimes the ultimate motive is placed in personal advantage, sometimes in social utility, sometimes in the love of virtue for its own sake. Perhaps with the majority of people the motive is nothing but the desire to obey a generally accepted rule. The Greek word "ethic" is closely allied to the word for "custom," and reflects the idea that a man who lives rightly is one who is faithful to all traditional ways. In Judaism, as in most ancient systems, a religious sanction was added to this idea. It was assumed that the traditional law had been divinely given. Why God had so commanded it was not for men to enquire. It was enough to know that this was God's will, revealed to men in a distant past, and that He would punish those who departed from it.

For Jesus also the motive of right action was a religious one, but in a different sense from what it had hitherto been. Indeed it was just at this point that he broke with the religion of his time. Hitherto the .act of obedience to the divine command had been sufficient. So long as you obeyed God, whether from love or fear or habit or hope for recompense, you were acting rightly. Jesus transformed this outward submission into an inward one. He taught that you cannot truly obey God unless you believe in Him as your Father and desire to be like Him. He is the righteous God, and you can feel that in acting

[3]Matt. 5:45.

righteously you act as He does. The end of your being is to resemble God your Father, and you attain this end by doing right.

For Jesus, therefore, the motive of right action is to become like God, to possess in oneself more of God's own nature. Jesus has much to say of the benefits conferred on others, of the joy and satisfaction which a man secures for himself, by doing what is right. All these, however, are subsidiary ends. The grand purpose is always to enter the Kingdom, to win that higher kind of life which is only possible by obedience to the will of God. It is often urged, as the most serious criticism of Jesus' ethic, that it is not disinterested. He never seems to rise to the conception of a goodness practised for its own sake. The emphasis is constantly laid on the "reward" attached to well-doing. Many attempts have been made to qualify or explain away this insistence on reward, which jars on our sense of the purity and loftiness of the ethic. But these well-meant efforts are all futile. The idea of reward is essential in Jesus' teaching. He does not conceive of goodness as practised for itself, and if he had done so his ethic would not have been raised to a higher level, but would have been emptied of its meaning. Our test of the value of anything is the result that flows from it, and are we to believe that goodness, which is the highest thing we know, has no result whatever? Jesus affirms that even when it seems to go for nothing it cannot fail of the richest reward, not, indeed, in any material wealth, but in the attainment of a higher life. By doing the will of God we become more like God, we win for ourselves entrance into His Kingdom. This is the reward, and the desire to obtain it is the one motive of the good life.

The Ethical Task of the Church

The point is a crucial one, for here we are to find the characteristic feature of the Christian morality. This term is often
used very loosely, to describe any kind of conduct that seems
to be in accord with Jesus' teaching. When a man performs
some generous action he is said to prove himself a true Christian. He may have been prompted by mere good nature, or a
desire for popular esteem. He may have had some higher motive, patriotism, a sense of duty, pity for human suffering. But
however we may admire the action in itself, and even the
motive out of which it springs, it is not necessarily Christian.
In Christian morality there always must be some desire for the
higher life, for fellowship with God. This desire may not be a
conscious one, for it is one of the marks of Jesus' teaching that
he thinks of the purest goodness as unconscious. The will has
become so identified with the will of God that it chooses the
right as by its own natural impulse. Yet no action is truly
Christian unless somewhere at the roots of it there is the religious motive. It is this, indeed, that constitutes the charm and
significance of a Christian act. Whatever its character may be
it is lifted out of the domain of selfish and worldly ends.
Done solely for God's approval, it represents goodness, without
alloy.

With Jesus, therefore, morality is not an interest by itself,
and to regard him primarily as an ethical teacher is to miss
the real purpose of his message. His ethic is certainly more than
incidental, for at least three fourths of his recorded sayings are
concerned with moral action. This is too often forgotten in
those types of Christianity which lay all the stress on doctrines,
or acts of worship, or mystical communion. Although Jesus did
not reduce religion to morality, he made morality cardinal, for

he conceived of God as righteous, and only to be approached by the way of righteousness. Yet righteousness is only the way, and the mind of Jesus is always fixed on the goal. His aim is to waken in men the sense of the Kingdom and the desire to enter it. They will attain to it by the practice of righteousness, but this by itself must not be their primary interest. They must feel themselves to be like travellers who follow the road for the sake of the journey's end.

"Seek ye the Kingdom of God"; that is the theme of Jesus' message, and he dwells on the need of righteousness because this is how the Kingdom must be sought. It follows that the righteousness he calls for is that of the Kingdom. Men must seek the Kingdom by doing God's will now as it is done in heaven. They are to anticipate in this world that higher order in which they will shortly have their part. The moral demands of Jesus are thus absolute in their nature. He looks to the Kingdom and makes no allowance for human limitations and the imperfect conditions of this earthly life. The moral law is set forth in its purity, as it will operate hereafter, when everything is brought into harmony with the will of God. It would hardly be too much to say that Jesus, so far from being exclusively a moral teacher, did not teach an ethic at all. The very purpose of an ethic is to relate man's conduct to the given conditions of his life. Aristotle was the father of ethical science, and supplied the pattern which has been followed in all later systems. Taking man's nature as it is, he tries to discover how man should order his life in the actual world. How are the higher and lower impulses to be kept in equipoise? How can a man co-ordinate himself with the society and the physical environment into which he has been born? This is the obvious purpose of an ethical code. It is meant to provide guidance in living, and must therefore take account of all the hindrances and disabilities under which we labour as creatures of flesh and blood. This, however, is not done by Jesus. He takes his stand on the perfect will of God, which cannot be fulfilled by erring men amidst the hostile forces of the present world. As Jesus sees it, this world is shortly to give place to another, and he calls on men to identify themselves with the coming order. They are to live now as if the Kingdom were already here, and in doing so they will find everything against them. They will be broken against the opposition of this world, which knows nothing of that higher law by which they have resolved to act. Nevertheless they must follow it, and by losing their lives will find them.

So the morality which Jesus taught was that of the Kingdom. He fully recognized that it was not feasible in this world. Again and again he declares in emphatic language that the present conditions are directly contrary to those of the coming age. The world as we know it is made for the powerful, the calculating, the self-assertive, and it is they who will prosper in it. They have the right to do so, since they belong to this world, and thrive in their proper climate. But a time is coming when everything will be changed. A new order will set in, and none will have part in the Kingdom except those who are seeking now to conform to its law. Attention has often been called to the paradoxical character of Jesus' teaching, and it is assumed as self-evident that many things which he said are not to be taken literally. He cannot have meant seriously that the poor and sorrowing are blessed, that men should love their enemies, that they should forgive without limit and abandon all earthly possessions. He only expressed himself, we are told, in the strongest possible language, purposely exaggerating his thought so that no one should overlook it. This, however, is to misunderstand his whole intention. His thought is in its essence paradoxical, for he made demands which in this world are incapable of fulfilment. His eye was always on the Kingdom, which was so real to him that he naturally took its law for granted. But the Kingdom which he contemplated and which he thought so near was still distant. The world of which he hardly took account was a fact, and was going to remain so. This was the real difficulty of his teaching. He called for an absolute ethic which, under the actual conditions, could not be put into practice.

At the outset this difficulty was not realized. The disciples were confident that the Kingdom was at hand; they were all the more confident since Jesus had now passed into the higher world and was sure to return almost immediately as Messiah to complete his work. They took all his precepts in the most literal sense, and tried to live by them. Their effort for a short time was in some measure successful. Every man has resources in him of which he only becomes aware in hours of extreme tension. The soldier in battle, the martyr at the stake, the good man struck by dire calamity, is lifted above himself and for the moment can do the impossible. So the disciples under the impulse of the Resurrection appearances were filled with a mighty ardour. The Kingdom became present for them. They could throw themselves forward into it and forget that they were still in the world. In that glorious springtime of the church the absolute ethic of Jesus appeared the natural one; all were of one heart and mind, and accepted the teaching of Jesus as the rule of their common life. But this outburst of moral energy was followed by the inevitable reaction. It grew apparent that the Kingdom was delayed, that the world was still here and was likely to remain. If the church was to survive within the present order, how was it to maintain the ethic which was meant for a higher one?

This was the problem which confronted the church, and has never ceased to do so. Christianity was the Way, and consisted in observing that new rule of life which had been given by Jesus. But how was the Way to be followed? More and more as it came in conflict with harsh realities the church was made aware that its task was impossible, and there must have been times when it was tempted to despair. The hope of the Lord's return had proved delusive. If the new ethic was in any sense to be fulfilled it had somehow to be adapted to the circumstances of the present world.

This, then, was the task to which the church now set itself, and which, on the whole, it performed successfully. Of all the debts we owe to it this, perhaps, is the greatest. The moral teaching of Jesus, in itself impracticable, was turned into current coin. The ethic of the higher order was made a working ethic for man's ordinary life. We have to consider the methods by which this miracle was accomplished.

In the first place, everything that could be remembered of Jesus' sayings was brought together and put into clear and arresting form. We have no means of knowing by whom or in what manner this collection of the sayings was made, but no doubt it was in process for a considerable time. From a comparison of the three Synoptic Gospels it can be gathered that short collections were gradually merged in larger ones, and that the phrasing of the Sayings was sometimes modified in the course of transmission. Yet a real effort evidently was made to preserve the teaching in something like its original form. It prescribed the mode of living to which the church was committed. Although it might not always be carried into action it had to be kept on record as authoritative. Those precepts of Jesus answered to the standard weights and measures which are laid up at the seat of government in a well-ordered state. All commerce in the last resort depends on them, and in case of doubt there must be access to the authentic pattern.

It may be safely affirmed that criticism has gone far astray in recent theories that the sayings attributed to Jesus grew, for the most part, out of conditions in the early church. The assumption is that from time to time the church encountered some urgent difficulty, and a solution was found for it. This was then embodied in a maxim or parable which was ascribed to Jesus himself, so that it might be valid for all future practice. In this manner, it is held, a body of teaching arose which was finally gathered into our Gospels and has been accepted ever since as the teaching of Jesus, although it had its real origin in the experience and reflection of the community. This theory has been worked out in detail, and scholars have attempted to infer from the nature of every saying the "life-situation" or practical exigency in which it originated.

Now it cannot be denied that some of the recorded sayings are plainly meant to bear a special application to the circumstances of a later time. There are various references, for example, to the behaviour of Christians under persecution, and in Jesus' lifetime the disciples were not persecuted. They were not "cast out of the Synagogues" but welcomed, and Jesus was allowed free use of the Synagogue in his teaching. The later conditions must likewise account for the obvious allusion to the church in some of the parables of the Kingdom. This is particularly evident in the parables reported by Matthew, and it must have been read in by the evangelist himself, for when Jesus spoke his parables the church did not exist. It would be easy to collect similar instances of how later developments have affected the record of the teaching, and this was only natural. The tradition, like a river, had flowed down through a channel which coloured it, but from this it is absurd to argue that there was no fountainhead from which it had sprung.

The theory as a whole can bear no serious examination. Apart from many other objections it leaves wholly out of account the most significant fact about Jesus' sayings. They are all spoken from an absolute point of view. Whatever may have been the occasion which called them forth, they are intended to state the rule which holds good for the Kingdom of God. In the present order of things men do not act by this rule and cannot do so; but here is the will of God, as it is done in heaven. It is entirely out of the question that such sayings were devised by the church to meet one and another of its concrete difficulties. What was needed for such a purpose was some definite, matter-of-fact direction, and this is precisely what is lacking in the Gospel precepts. It has been the chief complaint against them in all ages that they offer nothing but counsels of perfection. We consult them when called upon to make some grave decision, and all that we get is a general principle which we are left to apply for ourselves as best we can. The early Christians, like ourselves, were in need of definite guidance.

Ever and again they had to face a situation which was altogether new, and they would have given much for a finger-post that clearly pointed the way. If the church itself devised maxims for its direction it would never have framed such sayings as are found in the Gospels. There is hardly one of them that could have afforded much practical help. When they are not vague and abstract they advise a line of action which could not possibly be followed. No reason can be conceived for the preservation of the Gospel sayings except that Jesus had actually spoken them. For its everyday needs the church required such pointed counsels as were given later in the Epistles of Paul or James. But it treasured those precepts of Jesus because they were his, and expressed the ideals to which a Christian was bound to aspire.

Now and then, as we have seen, a saying has undergone some modification, so as to make it serviceable as a rule of action. This has happened most often in matters that affect law and discipline, where a general principle was useless until it was reduced to explicit terms. Jesus had said, for instance, that the marriage bond had been ordained by God, and must not be dissolved. This absolute prohibition of divorce was found in practice not to be feasible, and the qualifying clause was introduced, "Except in the case of adultery." In the same manner we must explain the curious passage in Matthew on the treatment of offenders. Jesus had said: "If thy brother trespass against thee rebuke him, and if he repent, forgive him. And if he trespass against thee seven times in a day, and seven times in a day turn again to thee saying, I repent, thou shalt forgive him." This is how Luke reports the saying,[4] and

4Luke 17:6.

it cannot be doubted that this version is authentic. Jesus will have nothing but forgiveness, free and unreserved. In Matthew, however, the saying is turned into a formal rule of church discipline. "If thy brother trespass against thee, go and tell him his fault between thee and him alone; if he hear thee thou hast gained thy brother. But if he will not hear thee, take with thee one or two more, that in the mouth of two or three witnesses every word may be established. And if he shall neglect to hear the church, let him be unto thee as a heathen man or a publican."[5] Here we have a clear illustration of how the church took liberties sometimes with sayings of Jesus. It did not put words into his mouth which he had never spoken, but in certain cases it defined his words and gave them specific application. He had called for unlimited forgiveness, but there were those who took advantage of this mercy and were a plague to the church, and grew worse themselves for the lack of wholesome discipline. The demand of Jesus was brought into conformity with actual needs.

In the natural course of things all the sayings might have been qualified in a similar way, for in every case they embodied absolute rules which could not be carried out in ordinary life. The church would have saved itself endless difficulty if it had quietly revised the teaching, and thus furnished itself with a practicable moral code, invested with the authority of Jesus. But it refused to do this. Although it was well aware that the demands, as they stood, were impossible, and that it was manifestly falling short of them, it yet kept on record the Lord's own statement of what was meant by the Christian life. Here we have the convincing proof that the teaching of

[5]Matt. 18:15-17.

Jesus has been preserved, substantially as he gave it. With every temptation to make it different the church allowed it to stand, although it bore continual witness, in those days as in all times since, against the behaviour of Christian men. The problem that faces us in the Gospels is not, "Did the church itself devise the sayings which it ascribed to Jesus?" but rather, "Why did it not do so? Why did it burden itself with a code of morality to which it could not possibly give effect?" The answer can only be that it never ceased to regard the ethic of Jesus as primary and authoritative. In practice it might be necessary to modify those demands, but they set the authentic standards of Christian action. Without them Christianity would lose its meaning. This has been the function of the Gospel sayings in all times. There is hope for a man, however unworthy his life may be, so long as he preserves, somewhere in his mind, an ideal of honour and goodness. There is hope for the church while it treasures, even as a memory, the commands once laid on it by Jesus. They have been often disobeyed, and in spite of the best efforts they cannot be obeyed strictly. It may indeed be argued that a complete obedience would be hurtful, since they were not intended for this imperfect world in which we must play our part. Yet the church must remember at its peril that in the teaching of Jesus it has true Christianity. All moral endeavour must have for its aim the fulfilment, in however poor a measure, of the ideal which is there presented. The early church desired to make this plain, and while it knew that the requirements of Jesus could not be enforced in the actual world, it preserved them as sacred. Every Christian was to feel, when no choice was offered him but to follow the lower rule, "This is not what the

Lord commanded; though I have done the best I can, I am an unprofitable servant."

Again, while the church acknowledged that the ethic of Jesus could not be fulfilled in the present world, it formed itself into a society which was separate from the world. From those who were within this circle it required a way of living which in some degree approximated that conceived by Jesus. It provided, in this fellowship of the church, the necessary conditions under which a true Christian life could at least be attempted. Paul admits that in intercourse with their pagan neighbours his converts have to allow for many things which make the Christian life very difficult. Whether they will or not they must consort with idolators and with people living in open vice. A Christian slave, forced to obey a heathen master, could not follow the dictates of his own conscience. But within the brotherhood the Christian rules can be put into practice. Its members have been selected and set apart. They are united in Christian service, and have bound themselves to encourage and support one another. In this fellowship of kindred spirits the obstacles to a better life have been smoothed away; the Christian virtues can be cultivated as in a walled garden. By its very idea the church was the earthly outpost of the Kingdom, and by living for the church Christians were able, in a sense, to live as in the Kingdom. They could endeavour, in intercourse with the brethren, to obey the higher law as it had been laid down by Christ.

It is from this point of view that we must understand the emphasis in Paul's Epistles and the later New Testament books on "brotherly love." Jesus had declared that all our fellow men without restriction are to be considered our neighbours; we must love even our enemies. When Paul bids his converts do good to all men, he takes care to add, "especially to those who are of the household of faith." The Fourth Evangelist, who is also beyond all reasonable doubt the author of the First Epistle of John, regards love as the very essence of Christianity. To possess love is to share in the divine life, for God is love. Yet the love which he has in mind is chiefly that which prevails in the Christian community. "A new commandment I give unto you, that ye love one another"[6]—that is, your fellow-Christians. "Greater love has no man than this, that a man lay down his life for his friends."[7] To all within the church a Christian owes a boundless devotion. This certainly does not exclude a love to those without, but it must take the priority. It must even overshadow family affection, for with his baptism the convert has entered a new family, which must henceforth be more to him than that into which he was born.

It is easy to criticize the manner in which those early Christians held together, and drew a line between their own group and the rest of mankind. This, indeed, was the principal reason why they were suspected and disliked in their own time. The pagans, with all their faults, were sociable and broad-minded. In the sunny Mediterranean lands they lived in the open air, and were thrown into constant intercourse at festivals and in marketplaces. More than ever in the first century, when Rome was bent on fusing together the diverse races of the empire, anything that made for division was strongly resented. The Christians were morose and clannish. They were wrapped up

[6] John 13:34. [7] John 15:13.

in their own small community, lavish in their care for those who belonged to it and indifferent to all outside. They were often referred to in a popular phrase as "enemies of the human race." Much the same opinion has often been held since, and largely accounts for the common aversion to the church. It is denounced as an exclusive body, concerned with its own interests and its own people, and treating the mass of men as outsiders. This is a prejudiced judgment now, as it was in ancient times, but there has always been a measure of truth in it. The church must needs be separate, as Paul pointed out, because in its essential idea it belongs to another world. If it allows itself to be drawn too much into the general life it forgets its own vocation, and those who have charged it with exclusiveness will be the first to condemn it as worldly-minded. Moreover in the early days it was fighting for its existence and could not hope to survive unless it was inwardly united. If it finally withstood all the powers that were ranged against it this was due, above all, to the intense feeling of brotherhood. Few in numbers and individually weak, the Christians were filled with the same spirit and were knit together in the closest fellowship. For this reason the church was invincible.

But the chief motive which impelled the brotherhood to draw a sharp line between itself and the surrounding world was that which has been already indicated. If the demands of Jesus were to be in any degree fulfilled there needed to be a sphere in which all the conditions were made favourable. Among men in general the Christian could look for no co-operation. If he gave way to others, if he was careless about his own possessions, his action would be construed as folly or weakness. But within the brotherhood the higher law could be put into action. Here was a fellowship in which all believed in Christ, and looked for his coming. They could try, at least among themselves, to exemplify the life of the Kingdom. They could exercise forgiveness and self-denial and kindness in something like the manner that Jesus had desired. The mission of the church was indeed to all mankind, but for that very reason it had to form itself into a distinct society. When a man of science has discovered a new principle by which he hopes to revolutionize all industry, he has first to work it out in his laboratory, isolating its activity from everything that might confuse and impede it. The church had discovered a new rule of life, and was confident that by means of it the world could be transformed; but it had first to demonstrate on the small scale what would some day be effective on the great one. It stood aloof from the world in order to make itself a sort of working model of what all society might become.

This has always been one of the great objects of the church. We are often told, and no doubt with some truth, that the Christian ideal of a world ruled wholly by the highest law is nothing but a dream. The lower impulses are too strong. In the future as in the past men will be guided by their self-interest and look solely to material ends. The church, however, offers itself as a society in which the higher mode of life actually has been achieved. Its members are united by a spiritual bond; they make it their aim to serve one another; they call themselves brothers, and think of love and goodness and compassion as the best rewards of living. Gifted writers in our time have drawn pictures of a future society in which all the evils which we now deplore will have disappeared, as a result of scientific progress and a better economic system. The pictures are imaginary, and usually, as we look at them, we are glad to assure ourselves that they will never be anything more. But without any aid from fancy it is possible to throw our minds into the future and see what the world may yet become. The church may be sadly imperfect, but it does, in the plainest manner, foreshadow a time when there will be no false divisions of race and class. It impresses on its people that they should live for higher ends, and be just and honourable, and devote themselves to generous service on behalf of others. The aim of the church is to realize in its own fellowship the conditions which may some day prevail everywhere. It exhibits in concrete form, and in the world of today, what we often think of as a vain dream.

By means of the church, therefore, the ethic of Jesus was made actual. In its full extent it could be realized only in the Kingdom, and was alien, by its nature, to this world; but a community was formed which tried as far as possible to model itself on the Kingdom. This fellowship of the saints kept separate, so that it might be free from the distracting influences which were always thwarting the law of Christ. Within its borders the new principles could be put into action. They seemed to the common eye to be visionary, but here was a body of men and women who were living by them, and in doing so had found a freedom and a happiness of which they had formerly known nothing. The church was thus a standing challenge to the outside world. Might it not be that this rule of love which had justified itself in the Christian community would produce the same result if it were accepted by the whole race of men?

The church thus set itself to exemplify the ethic of Jesus, but it also claimed the right of interpretation. Jesus had made absolute demands, and in their full import they were just as impracticable for members of the church as for those outside of it. All possible means were offered within the society for making the Christian life normal and attractive, and yet it was found that after baptism men were much the same as before. More than ever when the ecstatic mood of the early days had ceased, the old weaknesses reasserted themselves. Paul has bitter complaints to make of the moral conditions in every church he writes to, and it has sometimes been argued that those converts of whom he was so proud had not become Christians at all. Under a thin veneer of Christian belief they were still pagans at heart, with the old vices and egoisms as active in them as ever. This is certainly not true. Paul knew what he was saying when he told the Corinthians that they had been washed, they had been sanctified, they had been justified.[8] The trouble was not that they were still pagans but that they were still men, who found, like ourselves, that the Christian law was beyond them. They could not fulfil it, however the church might assist them, unless allowances were made for their human weakness and for the earthly forces which held them down.

The church, therefore, took on itself the authority to interpret the will of Christ. This is the meaning of the famous passage: "Thou art Peter, and on this rock I will build my church. And I will give thee the keys of the Kingdom of heaven, and whatsoever thou shalt loose on earth shall be loosed in heaven, and whatsoever thou shalt bind on earth shall be bound in heaven."[9] We have seen that in their present form these words cannot have been spoken by Jesus. How they

[8] I Cor. 6:11. [9] Matt. 16:18, 19.

originated, and what is their precise application will always be matters of dispute, but the main purpose of the verses is sufficiently clear. Peter is taken as the representative of the church, which declares that it has authority to explain the demands of Jesus, and to decide in what manner they shall be obeyed. In themselves they are general and indefinite, ideal principles and not formal rules. It is the duty of the church to relate them from time to time to changing needs and circumstances, ensuring that the lives of Christians will be conformable, at least in spirit, to the will of Christ.

In the Epistles of Paul we have concrete examples of how this work of interpretation was carried out. Paul has to deal with problems and conditions such as Jesus himself had never contemplated. His mission is to Gentiles, living in great cosmopolitan cities, and for the questions addressed to him he can find no direct answer in the precepts of Jesus. He hardly ever quotes these precepts, and even when he plainly has them in mind he only takes the idea and expresses it in his own way. Believing that he possesses the Spirit, that he is an Apostle speaking in the name of the church, he undertakes to bind and loose, pointing out to his converts how they must act on particular occasions if they would be faithful to the Christian law. We feel, in almost every instance, that Paul's judgment is sound. The course of action which he advocates is that which best accords with Christian principles. If Jesus himself had been called on to answer those questions which had arisen in Corinth or Philippi he would have decided much as Paul does. But it is also true that ever and again Paul qualifies the strict demands of Jesus. He does not look solely to the absolute moral law but allows for what is feasible and prudent, even for custom and public opinion. He recognizes that the Christians are living, not in an order in which the will of God is everything, but in the present order, with all the limitations which it places on human capacity and will.

Has the church any right to that authority which it claimed for itself even in New Testament times? This has always been a matter of bitter controversy. Again and again the church has become tyrannical and has substituted its own will for that of Christ. At other times it has been unworthily submissive. In its interpretation of the Christian law it has taken so much account of human desires and frailties that it has given away almost everything. Reformation always takes the form of rebellion against church authority. Some bold spirit denies that it has any real basis, and calls on men to throw it off and rest their faith on Scripture, or the word of Christ himself, or the inward witness of conscience. It has always been an ill day for Christianity when no one has dared to challenge the claims of the church. Even when they are acknowledged there needs always to be the clear perception that they are not final. The church at best is only representative of a higher power, to which every one has the right of appeal. Without this sense of a limit to church authority there can be no Christian freedom.

Yet the authority of the church was necessary, and has justified itself by results. It was, indeed, the inevitable outcome of the nature of Jesus' teaching. What he gave was the ethic of the Kingdom, and the question could not but arise of how this ideal ethic might be made serviceable for the world. Changes were clearly necessary, but who was to make them? The work could not be left to private judgment, for morality consists in obedience to common standards. If each man is to act on rules of his own making, the idea of an ethic is abandoned. There will no doubt be some who will act nobly, with no other guidance than that of conscience, but even with these all conduct will be arbitrary; for the mass of men the issues of right and wrong will be hopelessly confused. There will quickly be an end, too, of anything that might be called a definitely Christian ethic. Christianity was the Way, the new manner of life which had a character of its own. Other types of morality have always tended to be much alike, so much so that it is difficult to tell from the action of a non-Christian what particular religion he professes. If the distinctiveness of the Christian ethic is to be preserved there must be some authority to safeguard and define it.

Private judgment is not sufficient, neither can the decision of any one man or select group of men be final. Even the best of men can only say how he himself would act in a given situation, and his personal judgment cannot be accepted as valid for others. Paul writes as the director of his churches, but he is careful to make clear that he does not do this as an individual. He appeals to his status as an Apostle, an accredited spokesman of the church; in each of his Epistles he associates one or more of his fellow-workers with himself; he is conscious that he utters the mind of the Spirit, which has been given to him in peculiar measure. When he falls back at times on what he knows to be his personal opinion he frankly indicates that his readers need not be bound by it.

So if there was to be an authority, capable of interpreting the will of Christ, this could be only the church. The judgment which it pronounces is no individual one, but is the consensus of all Christian men, and what all are agreed upon is most likely to be right. This may not be so in scientific or intellectual matters, where the opinion of one man who knows must outweigh that of millions who are ignorant. But on moral issues, which concern everybody and which everybody can test for himself, the common opinion is seldom wrong. It may indeed happen that a whole nation, or for that matter a whole church, may be swept off its feet by a gust of passion, and fall into grave moral error; of this there have been many examples. But the church has a continuous life. In the next generation it can revise the judgments of the last, and in the course of its long history it has collected a great store of moral wisdom, out of which it can speak with confidence. This is acknowledged by the world at large, and the church, however else it may be regarded, stands out as the court of appeal before which all ethical questions come up for decision. A line of action which the church has stamped with its approval is generally accepted as the Christian one.

The task has thus fallen on the church of interpreting the mind of Jesus and presenting his demands in such a form as to make them effectual. This means, in almost every instance, that they have in some way to be qualified. If the world is to live by them they need to be tempered to the world's capacity. When we speak of a Christian ethic we usually have in mind this ethic which the church has evolved out of Jesus' teaching, and which is always to be distinguished from the teaching itself. Some reference was made in a previous chapter to the modern theory that what Jesus gave was an "interim ethic," not the moral law as it would be in the Kingdom but a law that men could live by in the interval before the Kingdom came. As an account of Jesus' own purpose this theory is utterly wrong; but the term "interim ethic" might well be applied to the later morality which was sanctioned by the church. Jesus proclaimed the moral law in its absolute nature, and it cannot be so practised in the present world. When the Kingdom comes the will of God will be done perfectly, but meanwhile it can only be obeyed in part. At every turn we come up against some obstacle, in our own nature or outside of us, which reminds us that we are still in the world, and cannot fulfil the law of Christ. In place of it we need to content ourselves with this Christian ethic, which the church has been moulding for us through all these ages. The principles laid down by Jesus are accepted, but at the same time are adapted to earthly conditions. We are subjected to the Christian law not as it is, but as we are able to practise it.

In this ethic sponsored by the church there are undoubtedly serious dangers. For one thing, it involves a compromise and this is always dangerous, especially in the field of morals. One concession invariably leads to another, until the principle which has once been encroached on is abandoned altogether. This has happened again and again in Christian history, and the church may be pardoned if now and then it takes an unbending attitude in matters that seem of little consequence. It has learned how easily the great interests may be sacrificed along with the small ones. A custom that was valuable a century ago may be meaningless today, and there is certainly need for some new adjustment. But in making it there is always a danger, for the trivial thing may be bound up with something vital. When the process of compromise has once started it too often means the end of a binding moral law.

There is another danger, and perhaps a graver one. In its

effort to adapt the law of the Kingdom to the present world the church is tempted to obscure whatever may seem visionary and extreme in the Christian demands. This, it might be contended, is all to the good. As Aristotle perceived, the key to all virtue is moderation, and the excess of righteousness, like any other excess, is apt to defeat its purpose. It is not necessary that all men should be saints and martyrs, but all have a duty to be good citizens and parents, honest in their dealings, truthful, kindly, conscientious. The church has tried to produce this kind of character, and to a wonderful degree has succeeded. But in its anxiety to foster these plain virtues, which it rightly considers the most desirable, the church too easily loses touch with greatness. Even the ordinary man is aware that there is something amiss and says, in his crude fashion, that the church has identified itself with the middle class. This, if it were true, would be no reproach, for the strength of a people is always to be found in its middle class, which corresponds, in the social order, with the temperate zone, the climate best fitted for the higher purposes of life. In all times, by its moral discipline, the church has tended to place its members in this class. But the real grievance against it is, not that it allies itself with a middle class, but that it favours mediocrity; and this, it must be granted, is too generally true. Christianity by its nature is a heroic religion. Its Founder was the supreme hero of our race, the Captain, as the author of Hebrews calls him, of all who have lived and died by faith. His ethic was that of the Kingdom of God, and is so lofty and exacting that the utmost of human effort can never attain to it. Men are all conscious of this, however dimly; and they cannot but feel the difference between the sublime demands of Jesus and the commonplace

The Ethical Task of the Church

morality with which the church is so often satisfied.

It is this mediocrity of its moral aims, more than anything else, which has estranged men from the church. Moderation is an excellent thing, but it is not attractive. There is something in all men which craves for the heroic and responds to it. Our human nature is full of strange inconsistencies, and one of them is this, that men who will not put up with some little discomfort will yet, on occasion, freely offer their lives. They cannot bring themselves to practise an everyday virtue which will cost them little and yield an obvious gain, but are capable of a splendid self-denial. The church has allowed too little for this side of human nature. For the most part it has presented an aspect of dull respectability. It has thought to win men over by keeping its requirements at a minimum, and in this way has defeated its purpose. Jesus himself made impossible demands, and this, in the last resort, has been the secret of his power. From time to time great leaders have rediscovered it. They have asserted the Christian law in its full extent, insisting once more that those who will not follow Christ to the death are not worthy of him. Not by weakening the Christian obligations but by making them sterner and more difficult they have touched the heroic instinct and brought new life to the church.

We owe a tremendous debt to those teachers who have protested against the Christian ethic as it is commonly practised, and have called for a strict obedience to the precepts of Jesus. Our religion is ultimately founded on those lofty precepts, and will crumble and fall if they should ever be forgotten. Yet the church, in its effort to adapt the Gospel teaching to actual conditions, has done a great and necessary service. Men are required as Christians to live as in the Kingdom, but the fact remains that they are in this world, and whether they will or not they must come to terms with it. When they seek to defy the earthly order they arrive, too often, not at a higher Christianity but at some kind of fanaticism. The church, in the early days and in all times since, has sought to make Christianity a working religion for the great mass of men. It asks for a mode of living which may not be Christian in the absolute sense, but yet accords with the Christian principles. Instead of a task which is utterly beyond them men are set to one which is within their compass, and which they cannot without shame leave unattempted.

The church has indeed failed at times even in this restricted aim. It has made doubtful compromises. It contains multitudes of men and women who bear only a faint resemblance to those first disciples for whom the invisible world was more real than this one. Yet it needs, perhaps, to have this miscellaneous character if it is to accomplish its work. Now and then there have been small exclusive sects which have applied rigorous tests and have expelled from their communion all who fall short of the very highest standards. It is not these obscure companies of the elect which have done most for the cause of Christ. The common man, aware of his disabilities, has been frightened away from them. Their own members have fallen into a mood of self-righteousness, and in the anxiety to preserve their holiness have shrunk from all contact with many whom they might have helped. A living church is always one which opens its doors widely. Every sort of man can feel that in its fellowship he will find people like himself, with whom he can struggle

The Ethical Task of the Church

forward to that higher life which is beyond him but which he desires. One might almost say that the church has done its best work by freely admitting those who have no obvious right to be there. An army gathers into it many unpromising recruits, but it brings them under a glorious banner and puts them into uniforms and trains them. Professing to be soldiers, they become so, and acquit themselves not unworthily in the day of battle.

CHAPTER IX

THE CHURCH AND THE STATE

Ancient religions were tribal or national. The god was, in the first instance, the guardian of the state, and beyond its territory had no jurisdiction. If he cared for individuals it was only in an indirect fashion, as members of the community which worshipped him. His honour was bound up with the victory and prosperity of his people, and while he sought to promote their welfare they made it their ambition to bring glory to their god. Religion and patriotism, in the ancient world, were almost the same thing.

For centuries the Christian religion had no connection with any state, and for this reason more than any other it appeared sinister and dangerous. It was a principle of Roman government that every people should be left free to practise its own religion. In this respect Rome was more tolerant than any imperial power before or since, and it was largely owing to this wise attitude that the Roman peace was so long maintained. But Christianity, almost from the beginning, was excluded from the general liberty. There was no tribe or nation which acknowledged it, and it could not therefore rank as a religion. Its legal status was that of a "superstition," and as such it had no right to exist. It was far more dangerous than any other superstition, since it was not localized but cut across all national divisions. Not only did it lack any state connection, but it threatened the whole idea of a unified state.

The Church and the State

This isolation of Christianity was due to the unexpected turn which its history had taken. The original hope of the disciples was to win over the Jewish people. They did not at first surmise that what Jesus had given was nothing less than a new religion. He had appeared as the Messiah, in whom the hopes of Israel were to reach their consummation, and the nation, although for the moment it had rejected him, was sure in a little time to accept him in his true character. The early mission was concentrated on work in Palestine, with a view to the conversion of Israel. When this was secured Christianity would stand out as Judaism, renewed from within and perfected, and would take its place with other national religions. This early hope was frustrated. It soon became evident that the Jews would have nothing to do with the new message. From mere indifference they passed to open hostility, and the mission gradually abandoned Palestine and sought new fields among the Gentiles. It had now to make its appeal simply as a religion, unconnected with any nationality. This was the cause of all its difficulties, from the time of Paul onward. It had to make its way as best it could without any outward credentials. Wherever it appeared in the Roman world it was much in the position of a man who sets out to travel without a passport.

This trouble was due, however, when we look deeper, to no mere historical accident. The nature of Christianity was such that it could not make itself into a national religion. This, indeed, was the reason why the Jews had rejected it. Their religion was based on the confidence that they were the people chosen by God. They clung to the Law, with its ordinances and customs, which marked them out as a race apart. No one was allowed the privileges of their faith unless he was a Jew by descent, or at least by adoption. But it belonged to the very essence of Jesus' message that he proclaimed all men to be children of God. Although he had confined his work to the Jews, he addressed them not as Jews but simply as men. His religion was inherently universal, and could not but break through all national barriers and find its way to all men, as water rises to its level. The Jews resented the endeavour to force on them a religion which denied their sacred prerogatives. Long before the Christians themselves suspected it, the Jews perceived that this Christianity was not Judaism. It was a new religion altogether, and must be left to itself. Wherever it went, men made the same discovery. The Christian message was incompatible with any kind of national restriction. It was alien to all the ideas with which the name of religion had hitherto been associated.

Jesus himself had never interfered with issues that concerned the state. This sometimes has been taken as evidence that his outlook was narrow and parochial. Living in a remote province he had never turned his mind to large political questions, and was, perhaps, hardly aware of them. A view of this kind is manifestly absurd. The time in which Jesus lived was one of intense political excitement. Palestine was already seething with the discontent which was to break out a generation later in the great revolt, and wherever men met their discussion was sure to lead up to the one burning issue of national right as against the domination of Rome. Galilee, for that part, was by no means the tranquil countryside which it has often been pictured. On the contrary, it was notorious as a centre of civil disturbances. The spirit of Jewish independence was warmer in that small province than anywhere else in Palestine, and in Jesus' own childhood Galilee had been the scene of an uprising which had been ferociously quelled and had left bitter memories.

It was in this atmosphere of political ferment that Jesus had grown up, but it is certain that in his teaching he held studiously aloof from politics. The reason is no doubt partly to be sought in the very fact that they counted for so much in the life of the people. Jesus' message was a religious one, and he knew that its meaning would be fatally obscured if it were mixed up with political debate. Moreover, any allusion to the vexed issue of national right would have been dangerous. If he had once committed himself to one side or another of the quarrel there would have been a speedy end to his work as a public teacher. His ministry was short, and the wonder is that it was allowed to continue so long; this was due only to the consummate prudence with which he avoided those perilous controversies which beset him on every side.

His political aloofness, however, is not to be set down to mere prudential motives. If he had believed that the national issue was in any way a vital one he certainly would have dealt with it, regardless of consequences. He held aloof from politics because he was indifferent to them. The one interest which occupied his mind, to the exclusion of all else, was that of the Kingdom of God. A day was at hand when the present order would come to an end and all the questions which now appeared so important would be emptied of meaning. Even now they had become trivial and unreal in view of the tremendous change that was impending. This, we cannot doubt, was the attitude of Jesus to the party conflicts and patriotic agitations of his time. He saw the men of his generation as children playing in the marketplace, so intent on their foolish game that they did not see the tempest that was gathering overhead and would sweep this world away.

On one occasion only does Jesus touch directly on the claims of the state, and even then he does not speak of his own volition. His enemies, in their effort to collect evidence against him during the last week in Jerusalem, asked him to say explicitly whether it was right to pay tribute to Cæsar.[1] However he answered he could not but put himself in danger. If he said "yes," he would alienate the common people who were his chief support; if he said "no," he could at once be denounced to the Roman government as a rebel. He eluded the snare by his famous answer: "Render to Cæsar the things that are Cæsar's, and to God the things that are God's." The answer has often been criticized as an evasion, and a somewhat unworthy one. Whatever may have been the purpose of the question put to him, it was perfectly legitimate and important. How can religious duty be reconciled with loyalty to the state? This always has been a crucial problem, and for the Jewish people at that time it was more urgent than any other. A religious teacher had no right to waive it aside by a platitude or a verbal quibble, which was all that Jesus offered by way of answer. But when his words are fairly considered they can be seen to meet the question in a clear and straightforward manner, so much so that they dispose of it definitely and for all time.

In that brief saying he makes three distinct pronouncements. First, he frankly acknowledges the right of the state. It confers

[1]Mark 12:13–17.

The Church and the State

certain benefits, and those who accept them must make a due return. This idea is brought out forcibly by the gesture with which Jesus accompanied his answer. He surprised his questioners into showing him a coin, stamped with the image and name of Cæsar. While pretending a doubt as to whether they should submit to the emperor they had his money actually in their possession. Since they availed themselves of what he gave them, they were bound, in common honesty, to pay him back. This is still the valid answer to those who enjoy the protection of the state and would yet refuse to do their part in its service. Again, Jesus makes clear in his answer that the right of the state is limited. It has control only in what pertains to the material life. The things that are Cæsar's are money and property, all that concerns man's safety and well-being in the present world. There are other things, which do not belong to Cæsar. Each man is a spiritual being, with a mind and will of his own, with duties and interests which pertain to his higher life. With this side of man's nature Cæsar has nothing to do. Jesus thus closes with his third pronouncement, which is the decisive one. Man's supreme duty is to God. As a spiritual personality he has part in another order of things, and his earthly life is only the means by which he can fit himself for his true destiny. Whatever authority may be granted to Cæsar it must never interfere with man's higher calling, which is to seek first the Kingdom of God.

The saying of Jesus is thus clear and comprehensive, and is fully in keeping with all else that we can gather as to his political attitude. He was indeed a revolutionary, but not in the sense that he wished to overturn the state. He required for the sake of his mission that the country should be peaceful, and

many of his parables would seem to indicate that he approved
the firm administration which enabled men to buy and sell
and till their fields in security and make plans and investments
for the future. With the existing form of government he had
no quarrel. He indeed condemned the pride and insolence of
officials, and the greed which made use of power for base and
selfish ends. But in so far as he condemned the state itself, it
was only because he saw in it a necessary part of the worldly
order. Resting on force and man-made laws and an exaltation
of material things, it was by its nature opposed to the Kingdom
of God. Some modern writers have contended that Jesus'
activity had a political side, which has been carefully con-
cealed in our Gospels.[2] Of this theory there is not a shred of
evidence, and in view of the known facts there could not be.
Believing as he did, Jesus could not have been a political zealot.
The nationalists, whose cause he is alleged to have favoured,
were bent on an earthly empire, centred in Jerusalem. But an
imperial Israel would have been just as repugnant to him as
an imperial Rome, indeed much more so. Rome was pagan,
and did not pretend to anything more than worldly ambitions,
while Israel was professedly the people of God. Even to pious
Jews like the Pharisees the nationalist position was the betrayal
of a sacred trust, and this would undoubtedly be the view of
Jesus. What he looked for was the merging of this world's order in that of the Kingdom.

He was indifferent, then, to the state, but the state did not
return this indifference. It was instinctively suspicious of him
and was directly responsible for his death. There is much that

[2]This view has been carried to absurdity in Robert Eisler's learned
but preposterous book, *The Messiah-Jesus.*

is doubtful and obscure in the accounts of Jesus' trial, but it appears certain that he was condemned on political grounds. The Roman administration in Palestine did not interfere in religious matters, and when the chief priests brought Jesus before the governor they dropped the charges on which he had been tried previously at the meeting of the Jewish Council. Pilate knew nothing of the nature of his teaching and had no interest in it; and the accusers threw all the weight on one fact, that this man had made himself the leader in a popular movement, claiming in some peculiar sense to be a king. It has been held sometimes that the case was probably disposed of in a few minutes, as hardly worth consideration.[3] The accounts, however, are all agreed that Pilate gave time and thought to it, and that he did so may be taken as certain. To a Roman magistrate, in a province of doubtful allegiance, a charge of sedition was a matter of extreme gravity. Jesus himself might be nothing but a harmless enthusiast, and Pilate was disposed, apparently, to regard him in this light. Yet he might be an instrument in the hands of crafty conspirators; his religious movement, as so often happened among the Jews, might develop into a political one, and the matter needed to be fully probed.

Pilate finally gave sentence on evidence which he knew to be insufficient, and for this reason he deservedly stands out forever as the symbol of an unjust judge. The function of a judge is to make his decision on the ground of facts, and Pilate set vague suspicions in the place of facts, influenced at the same time by a wish to gain favour with the Jewish authorities. Yet he believed, we need not doubt, that he was acting in the in-

[3]This is the opinion of S. J. Case in *Jesus: a Biography*.

terests of the state. His duty as governor was to ensure the Roman supremacy, and this prisoner, though he might be only a religious fanatic, was potentially dangerous as encouraging wild hopes which might possibly lead to sedition. The Fourth Evangelist says of Caiaphas that in counselling the death of Jesus he spoke unwittingly in a spirit of prophecy;[4] and this was still more true of Pilate. He perceived, however dimly and unconsciously, that this Messiah of the Jews had challenged the sovereignty of Cæsar. The state and the new religious movement could not exist together.

It was the decision of Pilate which determined the whole future relation of the church and the state. The Founder of Christianity had been condemned as a rebel; this was the one fact about it which every one knew. Tacitus, in the first reference to the new religion which has come to us in general literature,[5] dwells solely on this fact, and takes for granted, as a Roman, that this is sufficient. The idea was fixed in the public mind that Christianity in some way threatened the stability of the state, and from the very outset the church and the imperial power were opposed to each other. At first there was no regular persecution, and Luke does his best to prove that while the Jews were hostile the Roman administration was friendly. But even on Luke's showing Paul had repeated trouble with the magistrates, and this appears much more clearly in Paul's own letters. Christianity had started under political suspicion, and as time went on and its character was more fully known this was not diminished but increased. There was seen to be something in this new religion which was inimical to the very idea of the state.

[4] John 11:49 f.   [5] Tacitus, *Annales*, XV:38–44.

The Church and the State

All the New Testament writers are confronted with the problem of the relation of the church to the ruling power, and we can distinguish two attitudes, at first sight contradictory. On the one hand, the prevailing sentiment is one of frank hostility. Christians had asked for nothing but to be left alone that they might serve God according to their own conscience. They had gone out of their way to comply with all the obligations which the state laid upon them, and had met with nothing but rebuff and ill-usage. They could not but resent this unreasoning hatred and learned to regard the state as their enemy. This attitude is expressed most emphatically in the book of Revelation, which has for its main theme the judgment which God has decreed and will presently execute on the iniquitous empire. The writer thinks of the world as given over to Satan, who has chosen Rome as the instrument through which he rules. Rome, in the person of its blasphemous emperor, is the Antichrist. The end is approaching, when Christ will descend from heaven, destroy his adversary and establish a new order in place of the old one, which will be blotted out forever. It must never be forgotten that the book was written in a time of persecution, by one of the victims. Allowance must be made for a strain of violence, which was alien to the normal Christian judgment. Yet it commonly happens that in a fit of anger a man blurts out his genuine feelings, hitherto carefully disguised, and we cannot doubt that the author of Revelation discloses the secret mind of multitudes of his fellow-Christians. They conducted themselves in every way as law-abiding citizens, but all the time they regarded the state as their enemy and waited eagerly for the happy day when it would perish.

Over against this attitude of Revelation we have that of

Paul. He was himself a Roman citizen, and was proud of this high privilege. He was also a born statesman, with an instinct for law and order, and could not but admire the splendid achievement of Rome. Out of the old confusion it had created a disciplined state, in which Jew and Greek and Barbarian could live peacefully together. It had established a system of justice, and took care that it should be administered by honest and capable men. So for Paul, Rome is not the Beast or the Antichrist but the instrument of God. Order and peace and justice are divine interests, and the power which upholds them has been divinely appointed. Christians are to render submission to the state "for conscience sake," that is, as part of their religious duty. They are to pray for their rulers. They are to obey the laws, not as a matter of constraint, but with the sense that human law is a reflection of God's own law.

It might thus appear as if Paul were wholeheartedly on the side of the state, and passages from his Epistles have done duty in all times to impress on Christian people that they owe entire subjection to the civil power. But there is another side to Paul's attitude. He indeed acknowledges the right of the state, but always with the reservation that it is only temporary. His real opinion is expressed in guarded language in a cryptic chapter of II Thessalonians, where he speaks of the approaching end.[6] It is not yet here but is not far distant; and will be marked by a terrible outbreak of evil, the supreme effort of Satan to destroy the cause of God. The interval is short and might have been shorter, except for a barrier which stands in the way. There is a power that holds back the forces of evil, which are now mounting to a fury. When this power is removed, Satan

[6]II Thess. 2:3–12.

will have complete mastery, and the present world will fall in ruin. Paul is careful to speak in riddles, but it can hardly be doubted that by the "Restrainer" he means the Roman empire. It has been ordained to repress wickedness by main force, to act as a massive dyke to keep back the anarchy from which human society has been reclaimed, and which is always lying in wait to engulf it again. This work of Rome has been beneficent, but is only for a time. The "Restrainer" will shortly disappear, the empire is doomed to fall. Here we are to find Paul's real estimate of the civil power. He sees that it is necessary, and bids the Christians respect and maintain it, but he allows it nothing but a temporary place. God requires that there should be order, even in a world that is intrinsically evil, and for this reason he has appointed the state to act for him. Nevertheless its title is valid only for the interval before the true Kingdom will come in.

Paul's attitude is thus essentially that of Jesus himself, as revealed in the saying on the tribute money. Cæsar must have his due. Christians are to submit to authority, and to regard it as just and necessary, but always on the condition that they do not accept it as final. They are to live for the Kingdom of God, and to realize that in their inner life they already belong to it. If there is any conflict between the two loyalties to God and to Cæsar, they must not hesitate as to which has the prior claim. Paul, in fact, is in ultimate agreement with the view which dominates the book of Revelation. Although he does not condemn the state as evil he recognizes, like John, that it is bound up with the present order and is one of the old things which will pass away when Christ appears. Our citizenship, as Christians, is in heaven.

One thing is noteworthy in all the New Testament references to the state, even in those passages of Paul which call on Christians to honour and support it. The obedience which is enjoined is all of a passive nature. Taxes are to be paid, laws are to be respected, rulers are to be held in reverence for the sake of their office. But there is no suggestion that Christians are actively to assist the state. We now consider it one of the normal Christian duties to participate, as opportunity offers, in the direction of public affairs. The church must interest itself in the general life of the community. It must point the way to better legislation; it must do what it can to humanize commerce and industry; it must lift up its voice against all aggression and selfish policy. We demand of Christian men that wherever possible they should take their place as leaders in the national and civic and economic life; if this is denied them they should at least be vigilant citizens, always conscious of their responsibility for the common welfare.

Of all this there is nothing in the New Testament. One reason no doubt is that the church in that early time was so inconsiderable that it could exert no influence on the conduct of affairs. Moreover, under the Roman system, all government was in the hands of an official class, which would brook no interference from the outside. If Christians had tried to meddle in politics, or had even drawn up a protest against some abuse, they would only have brought disaster on the church, confirming those suspicions of its character which it was most anxious to allay. Apart, however, from such practical difficulties, the church, in view of its principles, could not render to the state anything but a passive obedience. Looking for the Kingdom which was to come, it stood aloof from the world. To be sure, it had still to remain there, but this could be only for a time and all that was required was patient endurance until the interval of waiting was over. The state, on the other hand, was the power of this world. It might be necessary and beneficent, as Paul was willing to admit, and Christians would do well to support it. In return for the protection it afforded them they must render it scrupulous obedience. But it was not for them to take an active part in an order of things to which they did not belong. They were in the position of aliens in a foreign country, who observe the laws and pay the taxes as faithfully as the native citizens, and are grateful for all the benefits they are allowed to share. They recognize, however, that they have no right to take public office, and must not be too free even in offering their opinions. It is not their own country, and their part is simply to comply with the arrangements it deems best. This, indeed, is the very illustration which is employed more than once in the New Testament. The Christians are reminded that they are "strangers and sojourners," that is, resident aliens in a land which is not theirs. They accept the order in which they find themselves, but know that they must keep their distance. They cannot forget that they are only here for a time.

As it grew apparent that the world was not coming to an end this attitude was changed. The Christians were now in the position of aliens whose sojourn will be permanent. Since this country is to be their home they naturalize themselves, and perhaps interfere too much with matters which they do not fully understand. Within a century of Paul's death we hear of Christians who held official positions in the state. We see the church transforming itself into a society which had more and more to be reckoned with in political affairs. Finally it entered into full partnership with the state, and in great measure controlled it. The community which had held rigorously aloof from the world was now an integral part of the world's order.

This alliance of church and state was helped forward by the ancient conception, which had never died out, that a nation must formally associate itself with a religion. Rome had brought all the separate countries under a single authority, and the external union had gradually become a real and voluntary one. Old divisions had been obliterated, and there had arisen a great international state in which men thought of themselves not as Gauls or Greeks or Syrians, but simply as members of the empire. But this vast society which had everything else in common had no common religion, and while this was lacking it could not feel itself to be in the full sense a nation. Attempts were made to supply the want, by blending all the existing cults in an eclectic system, by replacing the traditional religions by a philosophy, by making the state itself, in the person of its head, the object of worship. These devices were all artificial, and served only to accentuate the need for a genuine religion in which all could unite. Inevitably the choice fell on Christianity. It was identified with no particular nation, and this fatal drawback which had condemned it to persecution now gave it a supreme advantage. By its nature it was not a local but a universal religion, the only one which could serve the purpose of a universal state.

The union of church and state was effected under Constantine, without any clear perception of what it implied; but eventually a basis was found for it in an imposing theory, developed by the great thinkers of the Middle Ages. It was held that God had entrusted the government of the world to two separate powers, which were to work hand in hand. As man is at once an earthly and a spiritual being, so there must be two organs for the maintenance of human society. Material interests are committed to the state, while the church is sovereign in the spiritual realm, and between these two there must be a perfect concord. The mediæval world was built up on this conception. In place of the empire which had now fallen there was established the Holy Roman Empire, under the dual control of pope and emperor. Theoretically they acted in harmony, but in practice they were always in conflict, and Dante attributes to this division all the miseries and calamities of his time. He never questions the theory; he only complains that in their ignorance and malice men have frustrated the plan of God. If the church and the state will each keep its appointed orbit, if they will both act in unison, if there will arise a Christian emperor and a truly Christian pope, then at last the world will be at peace.

In various ways this has been the dream of many thinkers since. They have laboured to show how church and state might so co-operate as to produce the ideal society, the church supplying noble designs which the state would set itself to execute. But the trouble is that the two powers never can be brought to understand each other. As soon as they try to draw together, they seem to spring apart. Every possible means has been contrived to make them united, but the experiment has always failed. It seems obvious and necessary that there should be two institutions, one for the secular, another for the spiritual needs. It seems reasonable, also, to assume that these two institutions, each in its own sphere, may work towards the same end and assist each other. Yet in point of fact they have always been in conflict. With the best will on both sides they have never been able to see with the same eyes and co-ordinate their effort. For the last fifteen hundred years the world's history has turned on the unending quarrel of church and state. Why is it that they can never be reconciled?

For an answer to this question, as to so many others, we need to go back to that early time when the church came into being, in consequence of the message of Jesus. It began as the community of the Kingdom. Renouncing the present world, which was doomed to destruction, it allied itself with the new order, and in the act of joining it men changed their allegiance, and became, in a literal sense, citizens of heaven. From the outset, therefore, there was a radical antagonism between the earthly society and the church, and the earliest Christians were fully aware of this antagonism. They formed a brotherhood which was to be separate and self-contained, acknowledging no control but that of the Spirit, which would rule in the new age. Even when it grew apparent that the world's order would continue, the church refused to submit to it except in part. Its attitude was one of passive endurance. Although it acquiesced in the earthly government it would do nothing that might actively help it. The church must show that it had no portion in this world, and was waiting for the Kingdom.

Thus in early Christianity the opposition of church and state was accepted as self-evident. Thinkers and scholars have laboured hard to discover from the New Testament how the two powers may be reconciled, but however the various texts may be scrutinized and distorted the labour will always be futile. The early church conceived of itself as wholly distinct from the state. While it was submissive and conciliatory it looked for a day when the present order of things would be dissolved. So long as it lasted the state was necessary, but the church represented the Kingdom of God and the state this present world, which is inherently evil. The church could have nothing in common with the alien power to which it had yet to submit, if it was to maintain itself on earth. Its submission was only a part of that "patience of the saints" which would finally be rewarded by the great deliverance.

The state was conscious, however dimly, that this was the Christian attitude. It has often seemed strange that the tolerant Roman government was so bitterly opposed to the Christians, who gave it no trouble and were morally the soundest element in the population. The persecutions have been set down to some blind prejudice, or to the malice of crafty enemies. But from its own point of view the state was justified. It perceived that the Christians did not in their hearts accept its supremacy. Although they offered no active opposition they were enemies of the state. What we now know as passive resistance was making its appearance for the first time, and Rome was puzzled by the new phenomenon. It could see, however, that this want of sympathy might prove more dangerous than open rebellion and gradually undermine the strength of the state. The great persecutions began in the third century, when the empire, after long security, was faced by the menace of invasion, and was finding itself impotent. Something, it was felt, had been eating away the force and loyalty of the people, and what could this be but the new religion, with its insidious promise of another Kingdom? Moreover, although the Christian doctrines were little understood they were known to be subversive of the moral order on which the state was founded. Celsus, who made the first reasoned attack on Christianity in the middle of the second century, was a fair-minded man, who had studied the Gospels at first hand. He gives it as his deliberate opinion that those who followed the teaching of Jesus were bad men. They were humble, and advocated peace, and had no desire for wealth and power, and were friendly to the weak and outcast. But a man's first duty was to the state, and it needed citizens who would assert themselves and increase in wealth and make it their one ambition to be strong. This pagan recognizes, in his own manner, that Christianity stands for a new order, incompatible with the interests of this world.

For the early Christians, then, the church and the state were radically opposed. This view was modified as time went on, and the hostility gave way to an understanding, and finally to an alliance; but the primitive attitude was, on Christian principles, the logical one. The church exists for the Kingdom of God, the state for the present world; and there can be no real affinity between them, although they must live side by side. The state at its best is concerned with earthly ends, which must be attained by earthly means. It has to ensure its own security and assert its might. It must aim at enriching itself, if need be at the expense of others. All this is contrary to the Gospel teaching, and is yet necessary. As a power of this world the state has no choice but to act on principles which are inherent in the world's order. The question of war is the capital instance. There cannot be a doubt that war is the very negation of the gospel; and yet the state must be prepared for it, and is unfaithful to its task if it does not, on a right occasion, engage in it with its utmost might. However noble may be the purposes of a state it has to achieve them within the limits of this world's order, in which conflict, of one kind or another, is a primary law. It may be that some day the struggle will take a less barbarous form than mutual slaughter, but this is the utmost that can be hoped for. We shall always be faced by the paradox that great moral interests must, at a certain point, be asserted by what seem to be immoral means. What we supremely care for and believe in we must be ready to fight for, and the refusal to do so becomes wrong. The church, however, stands for an order which is different from the earthly one. In this higher order the material things are worthless. Each man looks, not to his own welfare, but to that of others, and the poor, the meek, the peaceable alone are blessed. For the state to conform itself to this higher order would be suicidal. It cannot exist as a state unless it keeps step with the earthly order of which it forms a part.

So between the church and the state there is a radical contradiction. It has been disguised in various ways, and can be at least partially reconciled. We have seen how Paul himself regards the state, within its own sphere, as an instrument of God. The world is evil and must shortly come to an end, but while it lasts it must be saved from anarchy. It is God's will that order and justice should prevail everywhere, and on this earth He has committed the duty of enforcing them to the state. The later church has taken up this New Testament principle, and has found in it a common ground on which it can co-operate with the political power. In so far as the state exists for great moral ends the church has felt justified in upholding it, even when these ends have to be pursued by doubtful means. Yet the attempt to harmonize the earthly power with the spiritual one invariably breaks down, and sooner or later results in conflict. As we look back over the last thousand years we can see that the state, at almost every turn, has found the church in its way, and has tried every method of keeping it harmless. Sometimes it has bribed or cajoled, sometimes it has persecuted. In recent years all civilized peoples have been horrified by the revival in Russia and Germany of those scenes of martyrdom which we had come to associate with the dark ages. It may be granted that these nations have indeed reverted to a condition of barbarism, but for their persecution of the church they may plead a real necessity. Church and state belong to two different worlds, and between them there is always a latent antagonism. When the state is determined to make itself everything it finds an unyielding obstacle in the church. This community which stands for a higher world must be broken before the earthly power can be supreme.

How can church and state be so harnessed together that they may work in concord? This is a problem which will never cease to occupy the minds of thinkers and statesmen, but it will never admit of a satisfactory answer. Anything but an external union of church and state is not possible, neither is it desirable. At various times they have seemed to be in full agreement, but this has always been due to a surrender on the part of the church. The evidence is written large in the history of the past that a church thus dominated by the worldly power is dead, and that it only comes to life again when it begins to protest and oppose. It is not too much to say that the true function of the church in relation to the state is this one of unceasing protest. There is no need that Christians should be hostile to the state, or return to the primitive attitude of a mere passive obedience. Since the state is necessary to this world they live in they must take their due part in it and work for its stability and honour. Yet they must never lose the consciousness that there is something beyond the state, and that its motives and actions must be judged continually in the light of that other order. It must perform its task under earthly conditions, and if it lost sight of them and looked solely to the higher standards it would come to ruin. None the less, it is these which the church must ever insist on. It must condemn the state when it falls short of them, as it cannot but do even when it has tried its best. This attitude of constant protest is a thankless, and often it might seem an unreasonable one, but if it takes any other the church fails in its duty. It represents the Kingdom of God, and can never simply endorse the actions of the earthly power.

The state cannot but resent the criticism to which it is thus subjected, often when it is struggling to do right in the face of great difficulties. Yet the opposition of the church is necessary for the welfare of the state itself. The worldly interests of which it is the guardian are inextricably involved with higher ones, and if these are neglected it fails even in its more immediate aims. By the presence of the church it is reminded continually that it is doing only half its duty. The protesting voice may be unwelcome, but when it is silent the state cannot be truly itself.

For one thing, it must maintain liberty, and this, in the final issue, is the sense of responsibility to a power above the present world. So long as men look only to some visible authority they are not free. They are in bondage to the will of a despot, or the will of the crowd, or the mechanical forces of nature. They attain to freedom only when they can feel themselves to have part in a spiritual order, over which nothing in this world has any control. "We must obey God rather than men"; this must always be the final statement of what is meant by liberty. It is the church which fosters even in its humblest member this frame of mind, and so makes him a free man. By so doing it performs a service which is essential to the very life of the state. It might seem as if the church were forever interfering with laws and methods which on practical grounds are advisable, and short-sighted rulers are anxious, for this reason, to override or suppress it. But the highest interest of the state is liberty, and this is one, in the last resort, with that faith in God which is guarded and sustained by the church.

Again, it is like the mainspring of all impulse to move forward. We read of ancient cities in which no change of law or custom was ever permitted, and this is the natural instinct of the state. Its one aim is to preserve what it has already, and it is nervously afraid of everything that might disturb the settled order which it has been at such pains in creating. There have been nations in the past which have endured for ages with nothing that can be properly called a history. The generations have followed each other, in the same round of simple aims and activities, never venturing on anything new. This, indeed, is the purpose of the state, to provide a fixed framework within which a race of men can maintain its own character and traditions, and when changes take place they are due, not to voluntary action, but to forces from without which break in on the accepted order. The church is a force of this kind which

is constantly operative. It keeps judging the life of the state by
other standards. It denies the value of possessions and achievements on which the state is wont to pride itself. There is thus
a contact not merely with a different culture but with a different world, a cross-fertilization of the earthly order of things
with the higher, spiritual one. The state is intolerant of the
church, which troubles its self-complacency and makes men dis-
satisfied with the conditions under which they live. But this
discontent is the motive power of all progress. It may be said
confidently that the advances of the last centuries would never
have been dreamed of had it not been that the church kept
constantly before men's eyes the vision of the Kingdom of
God. Whatever was accomplished there was always the desire for something better. Out of this striving towards a world
other than that which we know, all progress has ultimately
sprung.

Once more, it is the church, with its message of the Kingdom, which gives meaning to the life of the state. In the natural order there is no purpose. The stars go round forever;
plants and animals endlessly reproduce their kind. It is only
in the life of man that purpose reveals itself. This, indeed, is
the distinctive quality of man, that his work is consciously
directed to an object, and the worth of his life is measured by
the nature of the object for which he labours. If it is to have a
real value the purpose must, in some sense, be a spiritual one.
This is vouched for by the universal experience that material
things, as soon as they are gained, prove empty. Every age has
echoed the cry of Ecclesiastes, "Vanity of vanities, all is vanity."
Riches, honours, pleasures, appear at a distance to be satisfying, but the moment they are attained the virtue goes out of

them. This is no moral platitude but the grim fact which makes half the tragedy of human life.

And as it is with individual men, so with the community. It has value and meaning only as it works towards a purpose, and the purpose must be a spiritual one. There have been great empires which have come and gone, leaving hardly a name behind them. They aimed at nothing but their own aggrandizement or material well-being, and with all their industry and conquest they accomplished nothing. There have been small nations which seemed to be of no account, and will yet be remembered and revered forever. They were dedicated to some high purpose, to the quest for truth, for beauty, for righteousness, and all that they did has for this reason a lasting significance. So it is the function of the state not merely to maintain itself but to keep before it a spiritual purpose. Without this it is no true state; its existence is futile; its tumultuous doings will appear in retrospect to be nothing but the idle play of waves upon the beach. The church ensures for the state that it is living for a purpose. Its activities may be the common, earthly ones, but they are linked up with the endeavour towards something higher. They have substance in them, and contribute to the final purpose for which man exists on earth.

Between the church and the state there is thus a real relation, but it does not consist in an alliance which will enable them to act in unison. The relation is rather one of opposition, and it is this which constitutes its value. Jesus declared that this world is soon to come to an end and that men should look for that Kingdom of God in which they would find life. The church arose as the community of the Kingdom, and this, in

essence, has been its meaning ever since. In the midst of the
earthly order it represents the higher one, to which man belongs as a spiritual being. It is thus contrary to the whole nature and intention of the state, which is concerned with man's
interests in this world. The church enrols him as a citizen, not
of his earthly country, but of another, which obeys a different law. Hence it cannot but divide his loyalty, and must be
regarded by the state with a certain fear and suspicion. Yet
for this reason it is necessary. Left to itself the state would
be blind to man's true nature, and would fail even in its
limited task of providing for his earthly welfare. It needs
always to have this other power over against it, which reminds
it that its authority is partial and continues only for a time.

CHAPTER X

CONCLUSION

Before the end of the first century a movement had begun which was to divide the church for several generations. According to the Gnostic teachers the material world was wholly evil and had arisen through some primal error or catastrophe. Christ had descended from the higher sphere that he might rescue the souls which were imprisoned in the realm of matter. He had made them aware of their bondage, and had sought to restore them to that world of light out of which they had fallen.

This teaching, involved though it was in a fantastic, half-pagan mythology, made a strong appeal to many of the most earnest Christian minds, and it is hard at first sight to account for this attraction. Perhaps it lay chiefly in this—that Gnosticism appeared in its own fashion to reassert the genuine Christian belief, which was in danger of being thrust into the background. Jesus had proclaimed the Kingdom of God and had required of men that they should break with this world, which was unreal and was now nearing its end. The church had been unfaithful to this message. It had given up the hope of the Kingdom as an illusion, and was seeking to reconcile itself to the world.

The Gnostic movement was overcome, but the protest implied in it has been repeated in ever new forms, and is familiar to us at the present day. Later Christianity, we are told, has been nothing but a confession of defeat. The church has been engaged in the hopeless task of facing both ways. It clings, at least formally, to the original hope for the Kingdom, and is careful all the time to make terms with the world. Secretly aware that its hope is baseless, it refuses to abandon it, and yet in practice accepts the worldly order as the real one. This, it is alleged, is the weakness of Christianity as compared with other religions, or substitutes for religion. They may not profess so much, but they take life honestly, with all its limitations, and are content that it should be well-ordered and that human beings, while they live, should enjoy a reasonable happiness. Even this restricted aim may be difficult to attain, but it does not entail the doubt and failure and disillusionment which cannot but await us as Christians.

It may be answered, however, that the church was not driven to its later attitude by any sense of defeat. When the Kingdom failed to come, in the years that followed Jesus' death, the disciples did not conclude that they had been mistaken. They only inferred that they had misunderstood the "little time" of which he had spoken. His promise of the Kingdom still held good, but it would be necessary, perhaps for ages, to reckon with the present world; and its claims must be duly acknowledged. It was realized, too, that while he had spoken in apocalyptic language, he was thinking not so much of two ages as of two worlds, the visible, material one and the higher spiritual world which is over against it. So it was not owing to any inconsistency that the church continued to preserve its early belief. All that it did was to recognize that two facts are equally certain. The present order of things is real, so also is the Kingdom of God, of which Jesus had spoken.

How can we do our part in this world, and yet live for the Kingdom? Almost from the beginning the church was faced with this problem, and has been striving ever since to find its solution.

The problem might have been evaded if the disciples had simply withdrawn from the world and formed themselves into a holy community, wrapped up in itself. This was the course adopted in the various monastic movements of later times, and it might well have suggested itself to the early believers. Only a day or two's journey from Jerusalem there was a sect which had chosen to dwell apart in the wilderness. The disciples must have known of this sect of the Essenes, and perhaps their first impulse was to follow its example. Although they waited in the city, expecting to meet the Lord on his return, they remained a group by themselves. They shared their possessions and took their meals together; their meetings for worship were private; before the day of Pentecost they apparently had no thought of a mission. Why was it that they gave up their isolation and threw themselves into the world?

One reason may be found in the very confidence with which they awaited the Kingdom. The crisis was regarded as so imminent that it was not worth while to make any change. They were better to remain as they were, in the full assurance that all present arrangements were only for a little time. Paul develops this idea in a graphic passage of I Corinthians where he impresses on his converts that they were to seek no alteration in their worldly circumstances.[1] Those who were single were not to marry; slaves were not to desire their freedom; workmen were to stick to their occupation, whatever it might

[1] I Cor. 7:17-24.

be. The whole scheme of things was soon to become different, and to change one's mode of living would be only a distraction. "In what state soever a man finds himself, therein let him abide with God." This was the general feeling among the early Christians. Being in the world they made no effort to escape from it, since it was presently to dissolve of its own accord. In a sense this has always remained the Christian attitude. The believer follows his ordinary calling, assured that his part in this world is only provisional. He has no need of a hermitage, for his mind is fixed on the Kingdom. Sharing in the earthly interests he can yet sit loose to them, and under all conditions "therein abide with God."

Again, the position of the early church was fully in line with Jesus' own teaching. He had indeed announced that the Kingdom was near, and had summoned men to live for it, detaching themselves from the world. But he thought of the Kingdom in its moral aspects, as the higher order in which the will of God was done perfectly. What was needed for entrance into it was an inward disposition, a will in harmony with God's will. Jesus himself had "come eating and drinking." In all outward respects he had conformed to the world's order, and his separateness had been inward and moral. It is wrong to think of him as a social or political rebel, and it is equally wrong to class him among the ascetics who have despised the world. What he required was the new will. Those who possessed it, although they mingled freely, as he himself had done, with the life around them, were children of the Kingdom.

The Christian relation to the world was further determined by the inherent character of the new religion. It was not national, like the other religions of the time, but universal. At the outset this could not clearly be perceived. The disciples were Jews and had little outlook beyond the confines of their own country. They took for granted that Jesus had fulfilled the hopes of Israel and that his message was in addition to the Law. Baptism was conferred only on members of the Jewish race, or on proselytes who had been adopted into it by circumcision. None the less, the broader scope of the new teaching was apparent from the first. Jesus had limited his work to his own countrymen, but he had taken no part in their feuds and controversies. He had been the friend of publicans and sinners. He had not been a solitary like John the Baptist, who had to be sought out in the wilderness, but had himself approached the people and taught in their fields and villages. So when his followers continued the brotherhood into which he had called them they could not fence it off as a monastic group. Waiting for the Kingdom it yet associated itself with the ordinary life of men. All who would were at liberty to enter it. Paul extended his mission to the Gentile world, but he inherited the missionary impulse from those before him. The church had always been conscious that it was entrusted with a message which must be freely proclaimed to all men, and this was apparent not only to the Church but to the outside world. We learn from the book of Acts how new converts, even in the earliest days, were continually seeking admission. Gentiles were eager to join the brotherhood, in spite of the efforts which were made, for a considerable time, to exclude them. The expansion of the church, it might almost be said, was not due so much to its own initiative as to that of the world itself, which recognized, before the church did, that the Christian message

was universal, and insisted that all false barriers should be
thrown down.

We can see, then, how the church and the world were
brought together from the first. While they waited for the
world to end, the disciples remained friendly with it, not only
through the necessities of daily living, but because of the principles of their religion. As followers of Jesus they could not
but feel in sympathy with their fellow men. So in the later
endeavour to reconcile the church with the earthly order there
was nothing inconsistent. It answered to the original Christian
attitude, with only this difference, that what had always been
done unconsciously was now done deliberately. In the days
when the disciples were waiting from hour to hour for the
Kingdom, they still preserved their human relations with the
world around them. Now, when they perceived that the coming of the Kingdom was delayed, they took pains to strengthen
these relations. The church did not cease to be the community of the Kingdom, but it sought to make a place for itself
within the present order, and took on the form of an earthly
society.

This change could not be made without some measure of
compromise. Adapting itself to the existing conditions, the
church consented in practice to much that was alien to it in
theory. Paul admits to the Corinthians that if they strictly fulfilled their calling they would need to go out of the world
altogether; and he can do no more than enjoin on them that
within their own brotherhood they must try to follow the
higher rule.[2] Even with this restriction he is careful not to de-

[2]I Cor. 5:9-11.

mand too much. He makes allowance for weak brethren and for those who are in circumstances of peculiar difficulty. He takes into consideration established laws, public opinion, social conventions, dictates of common prudence. One of his chief interests in all the Epistles is to warn his converts against all avoidable friction with their pagan neighbours. In the Pastoral Epistles, which claim to represent the Pauline tradition, the spirit of compromise is much more evident. The Christian ideal is no longer that of the saint or martyr but that of the pious citizen, honest and diligent, earnest in good works, accepting with thankfulness God's material gifts but temperate and generous in his use of them. Religion, for this writer, is the means of happiness in this world as well as in that to come.[3] He blends the ethic of Jesus with the higher pagan morality of his day. Fervently believing in the coming Kingdom he so interprets its law as to make it fully practicable in the world that is.

Popular Christianity has always been a compromise, and perhaps it is only in this form that the gospel teaching can ever be made intelligible. The Kingdom of God, for most people, implies a betterment of the present order, not an order which is radically different. Protestantism has been especially prone to a confusion between honest service of this world and service of the Kingdom. The principle was laid down by Luther that zeal in his earthly vocation is an essential mark of the Christian man, and the principle is in the main a sound one. But it lies open to grave misunderstanding. On the strength of it men have convinced themselves that by working industriously, often for selfish and material ends, they are in

[3] I Tim. 4:8.

the best sense religious. The success which attends hard work has been extolled as the divine blessing, rightly bestowed on those who have done God's will. It is worth remarking that this glorification of work for its own sake has no sanction in the teaching of Jesus. More often than not he speaks of work disparagingly. He regards it as simply the means whereby life may be sustained from day to day; when it is pushed further it has no moral value, and serves only to gratify pride and earthly desires. The demand of Jesus is always, "Seek first the Kingdom of God, and the other things will be added." When life is directed primarily to work for those other things it misses its true purpose. One cannot but feel that the so-called "gospel of work" has obscured for many people the real meaning of Christianity. It has been preached by Carlyle and other modern prophets with tremendous earnestness, and has been acclaimed as the one religion which is safe and practical. Rightly considered it is the negation of religion. It rests on the assumption that this world is everything, and that labour for it will serve as an equivalent for doing the will of God.

The church, then, tried to adapt the demands of Jesus to the worldly conditions. This it saw to be necessary if it was to maintain itself in the present order of things, which was likely to continue indefinitely. It saw, moreover, that if it was to prosecute its mission and win the world to accept its teaching, it had to meet the world halfway. No one can deny that this course adopted by the church was more than justified by the result. If it had held without any compromise to its original message it could never have been more than a small hermit community, of little significance for the great mass of mankind. It could never have accomplished the work it has done indirectly for the cause of freedom, for education, for art and philosophy, for the spread of a purer morality. As we survey the history of the past centuries we realize how vast has been the influence of the church in every field of human enterprise, and this has been possible only by its co-operation with the world. But it may also be contended that by this co-operation the church itself has grown more truly Christian. When all is said, the world is not a mere obstacle in the way of the higher life, but contributes to it, and thereby has a religious value of its own. This was urged powerfully by the Christian thinkers who assailed the Gnostic position in the second century. They argued that the world had not arisen in consequence of some fatal error, but had been planned and created by God. He had set His people in it that they might serve Him, that they might learn to trust Him, that through shadows and symbols they might rise to knowledge of Himself. If the church was to become fully aware of its own nature and calling, it had to accept its place in the world.

The church was thus justified in organizing itself as an earthly society, and also in its apparent compromise with aims and standards which fell short of the gospel teaching. Jesus had required an absolute obedience to God's will, and within the limitations of man's present existence this could not be. If the gospel precepts were to be carried into action they needed to be made practicable. Men cannot live in this world as if they were in the Kingdom, but they can at least keep before them the principles which Jesus had laid down, and try, according to their capacity, to follow them. It is easy to accuse the church of inconsistency, showing that in every age it has contented itself with the second-best, and has never lived up to the full stature of the religion which it has professed. All this is true, but surely it is something to have made Christianity a working rule of life. Only a few rare saints have ever been able to attempt entire obedience to the law of Christ, and even they have confessed their failure. Of all men, indeed, they have been most bitterly conscious that his law cannot be fulfilled. But millions of men and women have understood the Christianity taught by the church, and have put it into practice. The Christian life has been brought within their compass, so that they admit themselves to be without excuse when they fall short of it. The religion set before them may be only a poor reflection of that of Jesus, but it does represent, however imperfectly, what he had in mind. This, indeed, is the chief glory of the church, that it has made the law of the Kingdom effectual in the everyday life of the world.

In its ultimate nature, however, the church is opposed to this world's order. It had its origin in Jesus' message of the Kingdom and is nothing else than the brotherhood of those who live for the Kingdom. In the midst of the earthly order it stands for a higher one, in which all present values are reversed. The first disciples thought apocalyptically, and looked for a visible return of Christ and a sudden transformation of the whole existing order. But the apocalyptic ideas were only accidental. What the primitive church believed in was the reality of a higher world, and this, however we may conceive it, is still the fundamental belief of the church. It is the standing protest against the world as it is. It is always in conflict with the wisdom of the age, with the current morality, with the social and political institutions. The very reason of its existence is to condemn the order of this world, in which for the time being it must remain. All through its history, even when it has been most corrupt, it has preserved some knowledge of its true calling.

This faith in a visionary world might seem to be its weakness. It calls on men to look away from present realities and set their hearts on things invisible and aims which in their nature are unattainable. Almost from the outset it found itself compelled to qualify its message, and adjust the absolute demands of Jesus to actual conditions. In our days, more than ever, we have grown impatient of everything that seems merely visionary. So much has been accomplished by taking facts as they are and carefully building on them, that everything else is thrown aside as futile. The church, with its reliance on the unseen and intangible, appears to be nothing else than a survival from a credulous age. Conscious that it is thus regarded it grows anxious to compete with the world on its own ground, and gives an ever larger place to its practical activities. By devotion to man's welfare in this world it seeks to demonstrate that it does not live among the clouds, but has its feet planted, like other communities, on the solid earth.

Now it cannot be denied that all beneficent action falls legitimately within the sphere of the church. In the past it has taken the lead in every struggle for liberty, justice, relief of poverty and suffering. If it ever ceases to interest itself in these causes the life will go out of it. But most of the practical work has now been taken out of its hands. It has so far leavened the mass of men with Christian sympathies that other organizations have arisen which attend to man's earthly needs more skilfully and efficiently than it can pretend to do. The church can aim at little more than at imparting the Christian spirit to men and women who will train themselves, in the necessary manner, for all good works. There is one thing, however, which only the church can do. Its true function consists, as it has always done, in bearing witness for the Kingdom of God. In the midst of the earthly order it asserts the fact of a spiritual order, and makes it a reality in the minds of men.

The church is indispensable for the very reason that it concerns itself with things that can never be realized in this world. It might thus seem to have no value for the ordinary conduct of human life, but the opposite is true. Man is so made that he cannot pursue even his normal tasks unless he has a goal before him which is unattainable. The artist seeks for beauty, the scholar for knowledge, the saint for righteousness—all of them aware that however far they travel there is something beyond. It is this which gives meaning to their quest, and will and energy to persevere in it, for everything loses its worth when you know that there is a fixed limit. A theory has lately been put forward that the universe is finite. To be sure, it extends on every side for more millions of miles than there are grains of dust on this planet; but it is a circle with a line drawn round it, and somewhere at the back of the Milky Way it comes to an end. The mind instinctively shrinks from this suggestion. If the universe is finite, it is not worth living in; it begins to feel stuffy; there is no room in it for a man to stretch himself. That he cannot but think in this way is the proof of man's greatness. His life, as we know too well, is frail and transient, occupied with little earthly things; but he cannot live it without the abiding conviction that it is linked up with the eternal.

The church is rooted in this human need for a contact with

the higher world. It is an earthly society, subject to material conditions, but it is also the community of the Kingdom. It originated in those days of rapture, when Jesus had died and risen again, and the Kingdom was apprehended for a little time as a present reality. The group of believers, looking from hour to hour for the Lord's return, could feel that already they had done with the world and had entered on the new age. As the time of waiting was prolonged this mood of ecstasy passed away, and the church accepted the world's conditions. Yet it never ceased to be conscious that amidst the visible order it stood for the higher one; and this, in all times, has been the principle of its being. If the church is to live on, it must therefore remind itself, ever and again, how it first arose, out of the message of Jesus. The little company at Jerusalem has grown into a multitude that cannot be numbered, with interests so many and various that the central one is too easily forgotten. In those primitive days we see the church in its essential nature, as the brotherhood which waited on earth for the Kingdom of God.

A SHORT LIST OF BOOKS

The literature which deals with the early church, in its various aspects, is enormous, and almost every work of Christian scholarship might be included in it. In this brief bibliography the author has confined himself, as far as possible, to books which have a special bearing on the subjects he has discussed, which are accessible in English, and which have been published within the last few years. He has tried, also, to select books which are typical of different points of view, and has therefore omitted many which may be deemed superior, on their intrinsic merits, to some which are here mentioned.

Among older books which are still of the highest value are

Harnack, Adolf von, *The Mission and Expansion of Christianity*.
Pfleiderer, Otto, *Primitive Christianity*.
Renan, Ernest, *Les Origines du Christianisme*.
Weiss, J., and Knopf, R., *History of Primitive Christianity*.
McGiffert, A. C., *The Apostolic Age*.
Loisy, A. F., *The Gospel and the Church*.

On the early Christian history generally there have been a number of admirable recent books. It will be enough to mention:

Lietzmann, Hans, *The Beginnings of the Christian Church*.
Latourette, K. S., *The Expansion of Christianity* (Vols. I and II).
Moffatt, James, *The First Five Centuries*.

The *Life of Jesus* has been critically investigated in many recent books, of which the most important are those of the French scholars, Maurice Goguel and C. A. H. Guignebert. Both of them have been translated into English. The "Lives" by W. B. Denny and P. Gardner-Smith are on a smaller scale but well worth study. A book of special interest is Joseph Klausner's *Jesus of*

Nazareth, written by a Jewish scholar from an orthodox Jewish point of view. Conrad Noel has presented the Life as it appears to a modern Socialist. Mention should be made of *Jesus the Unknown* by the Russian Dmitri Merejkowski, a wildly extravagant book, but full of flashes of genius.

The *Teaching of Jesus* is treated in its more general aspects by A. G. Widgery, *Christian Ethics in History and Modern Life,* and by A. Wilder, *Eschatology and Ethics in the Teaching of Jesus.*

On Jesus' conception of *The Kingdom of God* there have been several recent books of great value: Rudolf Otto, *The Kingdom of God;* F. C. Grant, *The Gospel of the Kingdom;* H. C. Dodd, *The Parables of the Kingdom;* C. E. Raven, *The Gospel and the Church.* Nearly a generation has passed since George Tyrrell wrote *Christianity at the Cross-roads,* but it is still a book which cannot be neglected.

All previous work on the *Book of Acts* has been superseded by the great Commentary in five volumes, edited by F. J. F. Jackson and K. Lake. Apart from the commentary proper it presents, in the two introductory volumes, a vast mass of material relative to the origins of the church. F. C. Burkitt's little book *Christian Beginnings* ought to be read in connection with this larger work.

Little has been written on the specific subject of the Nature of the Early Church, which is discussed in the present volume. The following books, however, are all, in their different ways, of first-rate importance:

Linton, O., *Das Problem der Urkirche.*
Porter, F. C., *The Mind of Christ in Paul.*
Dodd, H. C., *The Apostolic Message.*
Macdonald, A. B., *Christian Worship in the Primitive Church.*
Carrington, Philip, *A Primitive Christian Catechism.*
Heiler, Friedrich, *History of Prayer.*
Loisy, A. F., *La Naissance du Christianisme.*

To these may be added the writings of Nicolas Berdyaev, *The Destiny of Man* and *The Meaning of History,* which indirectly throw a real light on the constitutive idea of the church.

INDEX

260
Dc04

DATE DUE

F	JUL 19 '77	Reserve SPRG. 84	
MAR 5 '64	SEP 28 '77	RESERVE SPRING 86	
F	OCT 7 '77		
SEP 24 '68	OCT 21 '77	May 4 '88	
OCT 10 '68	NOV 8 '77		
OCT 24 '68	NOV 17 '77		
DEC 5 '68	MAY 26 '78		
NOV 16 '71	OCT 16 '78		
DEC 2 '71	NOV 4 '78		
DEC 17 '71	NOV 18 '78		
NOV 2 '72	NON 90 '78		
FEB 5 '75	SEP 11 '79		
APR 14 '75	SEP 19 '79		
OCT 28 '75	OCT 1 '79		
NOV 14 '75	NOV 28 '79		
	JAN 30 '80		
OCT 7 '76	FEB 12 '80		
MAR 24 '77	OCT 5 '83		